SCOTLAND
and its
WHISKIES

SCOTLAND *and its* WHISKIES

MICHAEL JACKSON

PHOTOGRAPHY BY HARRY CORY WRIGHT

DUNCAN BAIRD PUBLISHERS

LONDON

Scotland and its Whiskies
An appreciation by Michael Jackson
Photography by Harry Cory Wright

Distributed in the USA and Canada by
Sterling Publishing Co., Inc.
387 Park Avenue South
New York, NY 10016-8810

First published in the UK and Ireland in 2001 by
Duncan Baird Publishers Ltd
Sixth Floor, Castle House
75–76 Wells Street
London W1T 3QH

Managing Editor: Judy Barratt
Researchers: Owen Barstow and Jill Lavery
Editor: Ingrid Court-Jones
Managing Designer: Manisha Patel
Designer: Sharon Spencer
Commissioned maps: Garry Walton

Library of Congress Cataloging-in-Publication Data available

10 9 8 7 6 5 4 3 2 1

ISBN-10: 1-84483-614-2 ISBN-13: 978-1-84483-614-7

Typeset in Filosofia and Trade Gothic
Colour reproduction by Colourscan, Singapore
Printed in China by Imago

For information about custom editions, special sales, premium and corporate purchases, please contact Sterling Special Sales Department at 800-805-5489 or specialsales@sterlingpub.com.

NOTE
The abbreviations BCE and CE are used throughout this book:
BCE Before the Common Era (the equivalent of BC)
CE Common Era (the equivalent of AD)

Front cover: The Spey flowing through the Grampians
p.1: The coastline at Brora, near Clynelish distillery
p.2: The Island of Mull, home of Tobermory distillery
p.3: The River Laggan, water source for Bowmore distillery, Islay
pp.4–5: The Sound of Mull

CONTENTS

SCOTLAND AND ITS SPIRIT

No nation so easily becomes a drink. In the spirit world, Cognac and Armagnac are mere regions. Historically, Bourbon is a royal house, but geographically it is nothing more than a county. Tequila is a small town, albeit also a mountain and a tribe. Scotland is a nation, although it elides effortlessly into the glass. What you taste when you raise the glass is the extraordinary landscape of that nation.

The world's drinkers do not ask for a "Scotland", a "Scottish" or a"Scots". They use an older vernacular. They seek instead a "Scotch", far more than they demand any other distillate. The request for a "Scotch" is enough, with no need for "whisky". On its own, the word can only mean a whisky, and specifically from that nation. Otherwise, it has to be followed or qualified by a noun, as in Scotch egg, an oddly impenetrable snack; Scotch broth, which is best fortified with whisky; or butterscotch, of which some especially rich whiskies are reminiscent.

Unqualified, Scotch is such a familiar name for the drink that in many parts of the world people do not realize it is a type of whisky. The Scots know, of course. They rarely ask for a "Scotch", preferring to call it simply "whisky", as if there were no other. Wherever it is consumed, the whisky of Scotland should be spelled without an "e". The same spelling is used to describe the Canadian style of whisky. The longer rendition belongs to the Irish and American types.

Whisky is an English-language word deriving from *usky*. That, in turn, is an abbreviation of *usquebaugh* (spellings vary), the word in the Irish and Scottish Gaelic languages for "water of life".

The source of this water was further east. People have brewed alcoholic drinks from water and grain since at least Mesopotamian times. The neighbouring Armenians produced a "barley water", according to Xenophon, the Greek historian.

The Greeks called strangers "Celts". The Romans called them "Gallic people". Geographical names

From the granite of the Grampian mountains ... the water of life in the making (left). It will be a winding, heathery journey to the glass. The Spey is the greatest whisky river. At Spey Bay (above, at sunset) it flows into the Moray Firth, which opens in to the North Sea.

recalling these tribes are widespread in Europe. A part of Turkey is known as Galatia. The term "Galatian" was used by the Roman author Columella in the first century BCE to describe the two-row "race" of barley, the type often preferred today in brewing and distilling. Places that were Celtic settlements are even today known for the brewing of beer, notably in Bohemia, Bavaria and Belgium. Both Poland and Spain have provinces called Galicia. Parts of the present France and Belgium were once known as Gaul. The French call Wales *Pays de Galles*. Scotland has Galloway and Ireland has Galway.

As habitation spread westward in Europe, the various invaders and settlers, among them the Romans, Franks, Normans, Angles (who gave their name to England) and Saxons, never wholly imposed themselves on the farthest outposts. The edge of Europe is still sometimes known as the Celtic fringe. A word thought by etymologists to be of Celtic origin, *Pretaniké*, and believed by some to describe people painted with woad, recurs in the Latin *Britannicus*. This word provides names for a north-westerly peninsula of France, and a group of islands of which the biggest is Great Britain.

Even within the British Isles, the more southerly and easterly parts gave rise to two Anglo-Saxon languages: English and Scots. (The latter is remembered in the writings of the poet Robert Burns and it is still spoken, especially in coastal Aberdeenshire.)

The Celtic languages are no longer widely spoken, but they remain alive. One group belongs to Brittany; vestigially the south-western English county of Cornwall and Wales. The other group is the property of Ireland, vestigially the Isle of Man and Scotland. Among these, Ireland and Scotland are the lands of *usquebaugh*.

Why "water of life"? Perhaps because distillates were first deemed medicines, a judgment that persists among some of us. Or possibly because the steam from stills seemed wraith-like to early observers. Better yet, the ghost was returned to life, with new potency, in the cask or bottle. A ghost is a spirit. A spirit can also be a drink. In German a ghost is a *Geist*; some distilled drinks are also termed *-geist*; and the spirit of the time is a *Zeitgeist*. The spirit of Scotland is whisky. The spirit of its time is one of national rediscovery.

The phrase "water of life" in the context of drinks is not uniquely Irish or Scottish. It occurs in other terms, such as *eau-de-vie* (used in French as a generic for spirits) and the Latin *aquavit* (still employed in Scandinavia especially, sometimes spelled *akvavit*). Vodka, a diminutive for "water", is an abbreviated version from Slavic tongues.

Most such terms originally meant simply a distillate, produced from whatever materials were local: in warmer regions, grapes (or other fruits); in cooler places, grains. In the early days, imperfections in distillates were masked by the addition of fruits, nuts, herbs or spices. Some such

Gentler waters in the Lowlands. This pond is above the Water of Girvan, in Ayrshire, the county where Robert Burns was born. A perfumy malt whisky called Ladyburn was once made at Girvan.

drinks are still flavoured, others distilled to near-neutrality. A distinction between flavoured and "plain" malt spirits emerged in the 1700s, the period to which the oldest of today's Scottish distilleries trace their history.

A whisky, or a whiskey, is a grain distillate, almost always including a proportion of barley malt. In most parts of the world, it is today unflavoured, but retains some taste from the water and grains that were its original raw materials, from the casks in which it was matured and from the surroundings in which they slept.

Nowhere is this more evident than in Scotland, which has far more whisky distilleries than any other nation, in a diversity of locations. A whisky may be called Scotch only if it is produced there, but that requirement is founded on more than law. The spirit's flavours are shaped by the landscape.

In Scotland, what the French would call the *terroir* is highly distinctive. Perhaps it was this visible distinctiveness that inspired Dr James Hutton (1726–97) of Edinburgh, who is widely regarded as the father of modern geology. At a time when it was believed that all rock was precipitated from a solution of water, Hutton maintained that certain forms had once been in a molten state.

As the Earth's crust cooled and settled, the European land-mass splintered at the edge to create the part of Great Britain that now comprises the nations of England and Wales. The part that is now the nation of Scotland splintered from the North American landmass. The two met about 410 million years ago, and the line of this early encounter largely follows today's border.

The collision of the two landmasses, the rocky thrusts and intrusions, the volcanic explosions, the glaciations, left Scotland with the most varied geology of any small country. The fire and ice were there long before they boiled copper stills and cooled whisky. Scotland's firths and glens, its peaks and crags, its long coastline, the resultant weather systems and vegetation, create a landscape that is gloriously perverse. The taste of that landscape is the barley of the Borders and the Black Isle; the heather, peat, granite and snow of the Highlands; the mists in the glens; the seaweed of the Islands; the autumn and winter rains and winds of the West.

As Europeans and North Americans rediscover the lure of the outdoors, Scotland is enjoying a new romantic revival. The Scotland that challenged the Romans, forged an alliance with the French and inspired Mendelssohn is itself being rediscovered. Today's Italians, French and Germans are finding on this western edge of Europe a new escape. So are the North Americans and the Japanese, despite the challenge of their own outdoors. At the end of a day's walking, cycling, fishing or bird-watching, they are very likely to enjoy a whisky as a restorative or aperitif. While blended Scotches combine the flavours of Lowland and Highand, river and coast, the single malts each represent their own mountain, glen or cove. Enthusiasts for malts enjoy that journey of discovery, too.

HOW TO MAKE FINE MALT WHISKY

1. Harvest barley of the finest quality (preferably from the Black Isle, the Laich of Moray, Aberdeenshire or the Borders).

2. Secure a source of water, ideally from a stream (known in Scotland as a burn). Streams on Speyside tend to be heathery, those on the Islands are often peaty.

3. Steep the barley in the water. Spread the moistened grains on a floor to sprout for about a week, and dry them in a kiln, preferably over a peat fire. (The peat is especially good on Islay and Orkney.) You have now made malt.

4. Infuse the grains of barley in water. The ideal vessel, rather like a coffee filter, is called a mash-tun.

5. Ferment this liquid (by adding yeast) in a vessel called a washback, often made of larch or Oregon pine.

6. Distil this beer-like "wash" twice, or even three times. Do this in copper stills, made to your own design by Forsyth's of Rothes, on Speyside. Heat the stills to boil the wash, then collect the steam and condense it, by running it through a copper coil in a tub of cold water. It is easier to keep the water cold if you do this in a high mountain glen. Although this may be a hidden place, a licence to distil is recommended.

7. Age the spirit in oak casks, preferably former sherry butts or Bourbon barrels, for no fewer than three years (ideally eight, ten, twelve or more). Barrels can be obtained from the Speyside Cooperage.

TO SERVE

A glass shaped like a sherry copita will showcase the bouquet better than the traditional tumbler. Avoid coloured or cut glass if you would like to enjoy the golden, bronze or amber hue of the whisky. A splash of water will help unlock the aromas. Do not use ice because it freezes the tastebuds.

WHEN

A light, sweetish Lowlander after a walk in the country or a game of golf. A flowery Speysider as an aperitif. Perhaps a salty Campbeltown whisky with your meal (take some water, too). A heavily sherried malt after dinner or with a cigar. A smoky Islander with a book at bedtime.

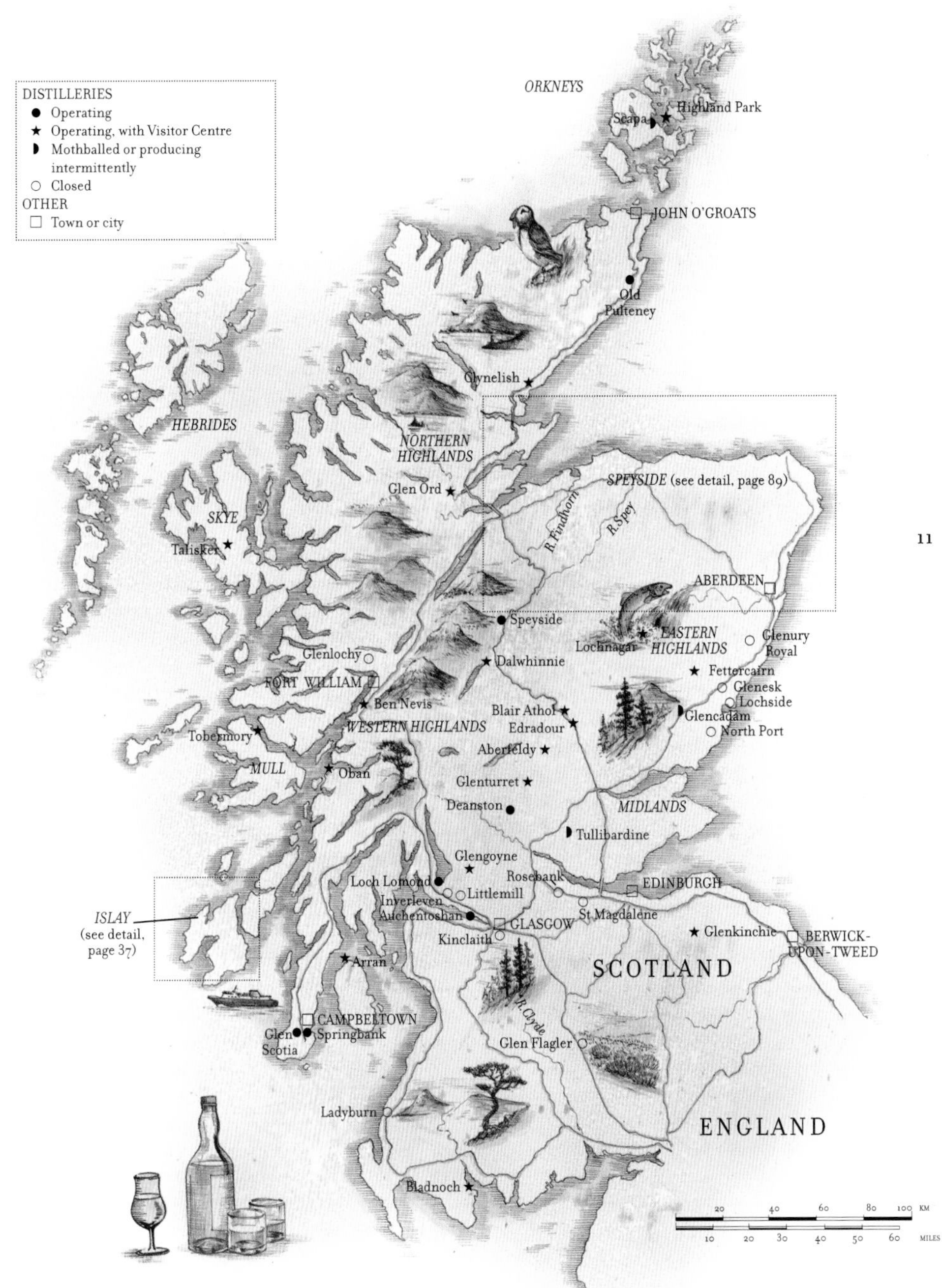

OVERTURE

Celebrating the birth of Scotland's national poet; a companion's journey of rediscovery ... a new beginning for a distillery, and for the Scottish nation.

In southern Ayrshire, the view toward Galloway Forest Park. The Lowlands produce whisky showcasing the grassy flavours of barley malt, without the peat and heather of the Highlands or the brine of the coasts and islands.

A LOWLAND JOURNEY

Wherever in the world one travels, the sea journey offers the greatest sense of arrival: the very edge of the new land gradually coming into view, people in silhouette waiting for the moment at which to wave a greeting.

On midwinter mornings, the short crossing from the north-east of Ireland begins in the dark, allowing the Scottish island of Ailsa Craig to rise with the dawn. The island, a dormant volcanic spike less than a mile wide, but 927 ft (338 m) high, serves as a greeting to Scotland. It may be a somewhat metaphorical salute, but it seems to excite even the passengers whose absence has been no more than a shopping trip to Belfast. It also caught the attention of such romantic poets as Wordsworth and Keats. There is an obscure symbolism, too, in the use of Ailsa Craig granite to make the stones used in curling, the Scottish sport that resembles bowling on ice.

The sea journey, in smaller, more perilous craft, was made by Celtic tribes called the Scotti about 1,500 years ago. They were by no means the first inhabitants of this land across the water, but they contributed its name. Some historians accord Irish Celtic origin to earlier settlers, the Picts, but that is uncertain. Even before them, Neolithic people of yet less certain origin brewed barley and oats on another of the Scottish islands (Rum), and left behind fragments of pot vessels bearing traces of this early beer.

Legend has an Irish giant using rocks in the sea as stepping stones so that he could come and show later inhabitants how to distil their brew into whisky. No one knows when either country first distilled, but documentary evidence comes late: the 1200s in Ireland and the 1400s in Scotland.

People have never ceased to cross back and forth between Ireland and Scotland. Wherever they come from, those arriving in Scotland today may be in search of lochs and mountains, music and literature, or their own origins. Or of Scotland's spirit. The water of life exerts a

A typical whiskyscape (left): the river providing the water; the pagoda vent (often retained even if the maltings is no longer used); the warehouses; and the village that has grown around the distillery. The River Doon (above) gave its name to the story *Brigadoon*.

powerful pull, which some of us are unable to resist. For me, a journey at the beginning of this millennium had a special significance. My travelling companion was a Northern Irish Protestant, Raymond Armstrong. Like the majority of his community, he is of Scottish origin. His surname is from the borders of Scotland and England, and his clan were once known as horsemen. A forebear, guiding his horse with one hand, used his free arm to scoop from the battlefield a wounded Scottish king. Hence Armstrong. My Irish-Scottish friend was fighting a battle to reopen a distillery that had been closed.

It was January 25, a notable day in the Scottish year. We were on our way to a dinner to commemorate the birth in 1759 of Robert Burns, Scotland's national poet. Burns wrote of love in a field of barley; personalized the grain as John Barleycorn, giving his blood; and pronounced that whisky and freedom went together. His respect for the common man made him an icon in the old Communist world, yet he is also celebrated in the most conservative corners of the Scottish diaspora.

One of Burns' poems famously apologizes to a mouse: "I'm truly sorry man's dominion has broken nature's social union." Quoting this poem, Armstrong told me that he had once failed an animal. When he was eight years old, his father had given him three sheep. While grazing, one had strayed, fallen into a flax pit and died. "I felt that I had been a catastrophic failure. I have never again allowed myself to fail in anything I have tried to achieve. I will not fail with the distillery." As he made his pledge, the ferry docked at the small seaside town and port of Stranraer, in the district of Galloway. So near to Ireland, Galloway is doubly a border region. Its southern edge is an inlet called the Solway Firth. The second word has the same origins as the Scandinavian *fjord*. Among the nations that regard themselves as being Celtic, Scotland is the most Scandinavian, not only in placenames and archeological evidence but also in its northern location and topography, and its strong element of Protestantism.

The Solway Firth has for nearly a thousand years formed part of the political border between Scotland and England. The two nations have had wars and border skirmishes, but neither ever conquered the other. Since 1707, they have, like American states, been members of a Union, but they have remained separate nations. At the beginning of 2000, Armstrong and I had plenty to discuss over the morning newspapers: new assemblies in Northern Ireland and Wales, a new parliament in Scotland, but nothing in England save the shared parliament of the United Kingdom.

The several peninsulas of Galloway are themselves like gradually larger stepping stones into Scotland. Galloway appears in geography and climate to be a miniature rendition of all that Scotland has to offer. Every corner of Scotland likes to claim that, but Galloway with more credibility than most.

Travellers love to discover tiny communities, hidden in valleys that seem to be time-warps, and in Scotland the sentimental story *Brigadoon*, on precisely this theme, can be hard to dismiss from memory. This Broadway musical and Hollywood film took its name (but not its plot) from a more robust poem by Burns, set around the bridge over the River Doon, in nearby Ayrshire.

We had a journey of about 30 miles (48 km) due east, into the heart of Galloway, toward Wigtown, which is not in a valley but on a hilltop. This was once the seat of a small county bearing its name. The old county hall is disproportionately grand, looking like an early medieval cathedral somewhere in France. Some of the town's wealth came from sugar plantations in the Caribbean colonies. The county has about a dozen big houses or castles, usually hidden among trees. A tragic love story set in one was the basis for Sir Walter Scott's *The Bride of Lammermoor* (1819). Another was the family home of author Gavin Maxwell, whose fascinating observations about otters were inspired by the wildlife in Galloway's rivers. Today, Wigtown is noted for its second-hand bookshops.

After 25 miles (40 km) on the road, we caught our first glimpse of the Bladnoch, a river about 20 yards (18 m) wide at this point, where it is crossed by an arched, whinstone bridge. The river rises in peaty moorland, then runs through plantations of sitka spruce, and wraps itself round drumlins in fields grazed by blackface sheep and Galloway cattle, some with a distinctive "belted" marking of white on reddish-brown. The waters finally flow into a bay below Wigtown. Even there, it is less than 50 yards (45 m) wide, but deep enough to have been a port, although its traffic today is the odd pleasure launch.

The higher reaches are sufficiently deep to accommodate pike, which annoy the locals by eating trout and small salmon. The lower stretches are fringed with native ash trees and reedy cover for pheasants, an easy ride for Raymond Armstrong when he wants to relax in his kayak. The mudflats around the mouth of the river, alive with curlews, pink-footed geese and Whooper swans, remind Armstrong of vacations in the Vendée region of France.

On the way from Ireland, he would pass through Scotland and England before crossing the Channel to France. He always stopped for three or four days in Scotland. "If I didn't have at least some time in Scotland, I would feel deprived."

Armstrong decided to find a weekend home in Scotland. Instead he found a whisky distillery. It is the only one in Galloway, and by far the southernmost in Scotland. It was established by a local barley-farmer in 1817, malting its own grain, and using water from the River Bladnoch. Like the majority of Scottish distilleries, it eventually bought barley from farther afield, and ceased to do its own malting. Again like most of its contemporaries, it nonetheless retains the malting kiln, with the typically pagoda-shaped vent. These structures have become emblems of Scotch whisky.

Some of the distillery buildings, all in local stone, date from its beginning, the manager's house from 1878. The offices have the look of a country post office. Behind, the distillery is set around a courtyard and surrounded by about a dozen maturation warehouses. It is a typical layout. The Bladnoch distillery, like many others, has been the focus for the growth of a hamlet. It sits by a stone bridge over the river, and watches over the local pub.

The River Bladnoch picks up only the slightest hint of peat, pine or heather on its way to the distillery. The gentle climate of the Lowlands has little influence on the condensation of the vapours into spirit or the evaporation from the cask. If the equally gentle sea breezes leave any flavour, it is slight. For those sorts of reasons, the few whiskies made in the Lowlands are mild in aroma and flavour, the grassiness of the barley-malt not masked by other influences. Each distillery has its microclimate, and that might influence the development during fermentation of fruity esters. The Bladnoch whisky has a suggestion of lemon. Perhaps even lemon-grass?

Like most distilleries, the Bladnoch distillery has spent much of its life supplying blenders. In recent decades, its whisky was a component of Bell's, one of the best-selling blended Scotches in the British market. In 1993, the producer of Bell's, United Distillers, decided to close Bladnoch. Its vulnerability was to be far from any other distilleries. Increasingly, owning groups like to put one manager in charge of three or four neighbouring distilleries. Had Bladnoch been half-way up a mountain, or on an island, its location might have made for an irreplaceably distinctive whisky, but Lowlanders are more delicate. Because whisky requires some years of maturation, a distillery usually has thousands of barrels in its warehouses. There would be enough Bladnoch whisky in stock to last for some years, and be gradually replaced with something similar.

Armstrong, a surveyor and builder by profession, thought the place was "a charming, wee spot". He felt it looked "friendly". He recalled: "When something feels right, I am hard to stop." The owners did not wish to deliver Bladnoch into the hands of a competitor, and sold it to Armstrong on the basis that it would be used as a home, not a distillery.

As time passed, he began to regret having entered into this agreement. "I realized that, yes, it was a nice, wee stone building, but it was also a distillery. It had been built for that purpose. It had a significance to other people. The local folk were at first unwilling even to talk about it, but I began to realize that their silence was eloquent."

Distilleries do not provide a great deal of employment, but even a handful of jobs are significant in a rural area like Galloway. More important, distilleries are a focus for tourism. Armstrong went back to the company and obtained a dispensation to distil in small quantities and sell the whisky to visitors. Although the principal equipment – the fermenting vessels and stills – remained in place, many ancillary items had been disabled or cannibalized. Armstrong set to work replacing them. The job would take the best part of a year, and entail considerable expense. In the meantime, he opened a shop at the distillery, and began to hold discos, wedding parties and ceilidhs in a part of the building.

Some celebrations of Burns' Night resemble a ceilidh,

The first Burns' Night of the 21st century, celebrated with due reverence and bonhomie at the Monreith Arms Hotel in Port William, near Bladnoch. This was a gathering in the more formal style – all-male, and featuring readings from the verse of Robert Burns, rendered with great insight and passion. Beneath his gaze, the toasts and songs continued into the wee small hours.

but the more traditional style is an all-male dinner, with readings and performances. On the night of my visit, 70 or 80 men from the area gathered at a small hotel in nearby Port William. The county veterinarian played the bagpipes as the haggis was brought to the top table. I thought of Raymond's lost sheep. Here we were listening to an instrument made from sheepskin accompanying a dish cooked in the stomach of the same creature. Later, a sheep farmer, adopting suitable costumes and props, performed passionate interpretations of Burns' poems. In a blend of tutorial and stand-up comedy, an hour-long tribute was paid to "The Immortal Memory" of Burns by the man who repairs washing machines in the area. It was hard to imagine a rural community anywhere else in the world demonstrating such a profound understanding of its national poet. We toasted Burns, many times, in Bladnoch whisky.

THE ISLANDS

Was Scotland's first distillation here? From the western archipelago to the northern isles, the pull of whisky proves irresistible.

The Welsh poet Dylan Thomas spoke of a ginger-beer sea. A Scot might describe these western waters as whisky-coloured, and dangerously seductive. Over the sea to Arran ...

The witches' tree of Scottish myth is the rowan, seen here as a backdrop to silver birch, tangled with honeysuckle. The rowan grows widely throughout the nation, but especially on Arran. In Scotland, its first syllable is usually pronounced to rhyme with a noisy argument.

TO CAMPBELTOWN

The upheavals in the Earth's crust that created the islands of the west left unfinished business. To be in Kintyre feels like being on an island. It is very much a part of the archipelago that fringes the Western Highlands but, by a mile of land at Tarbert, it is a peninsula, seeming on the map to hang precariously southward from the mainland. Even at its broadest, it is less than 10 miles (16 km) wide.

The Mull of Kintyre? The word "mull" translates as a peninsula or promontory. Though the phrase is often used to describe the whole peninsula, it is correctly applied only to the southwestern tip.

As Paul McCartney promised, the mist rolls in from the sea. Taking the main road can seem at times like driving on top of a dyke, with a sea of mist at either side. Sometimes, cows' heads poke through the mist. Once or twice, there are traffic lights to permit cattle to cross. The sense of being not quite connected is heightened by a slow, three-hour, 140-mile (225-km) drive from Glasgow, round Loch Fyne; for a crow, the journey would be less than 60 miles (97 km).

Many a whisky-lover, perhaps these days having first visited Arran, arrives by ferry at Claonaig (little more than a slipway) and takes the misty road 25 miles south to the distilleries of Campbeltown before continuing to Islay and Jura.

The sea mist seems to be a very significant influence on the flavours of the Campbeltown whiskies, which can be distinctly briny, but without the sharper saltiness of some malts from yet more exposed places. When the mist hangs over the town, it seems unable to escape. The town and its harbour are set around a bay on a curving sea loch, which is an impressive natural harbour, its mouth partially blocked by a small island. The loch faces east, back across to the mainland. The distilleries are in the town itself, in locations that are far

While the town (left) slumbers, the arms of its sea loch beckon the briny air. Small wonder its justly renowned whiskies taste salty. Do the whin bushes around Crosshill (above) confer a coconutty oiliness to the whiskies of Campbeltown? Or does that come later?

more urban than is usual. No mountain glens or hidden coves for them.

The town takes its name from one of the Campbell earls, supporters of the Protestant cause in the religious struggles that have characterized Scottish history. In the 1600s, Protestant settlers from the Scottish Lowlands became influential in an area that had previously been a Gaelic-speaking Highland community named after St Ciaran. There is documentary evidence of barley being grown for malting, and of distilling, in that century. If the Lowlanders were keen to spread their commercial activities into the Highlands, Campbeltown was relatively convenient in those days: travel was by sea, and paradoxically more direct, before McAdam's roads, Telford's canals and bridges or Stephenson's railways.

Campbeltown was a centre of commercial distilling before the northeasterly rival region of Speyside. It belonged to the steamship era, while Speyside owed more to the steam railway. The Campbeltown area was said to have 32 licensed stills as early as 1759. They reputedly had big, fat, onion-shaped stills, and that generous outline persists in the survivors, producing quite oily spirits. Campbeltown's decline allegedly happened after the distillers there became known for rough whiskies supplied to American speakeasies during Prohibition.

Latterly, all the distilleries took their water from the same source, which is unusual. The source, a couple of miles south of the town, is a dammed loch, a few hundred yards long, in the foothills of Beinn Ghuilean. Crosshill Loch is in a setting high enough to offer views of both Arran and Islay. With the sea at both sides, the air can be as fresh as an incoming tide. When the whin is in blossom, it is also heavy with the coconut-like perfume of the surrounding bushes. Perhaps that is the origin of the distinctive coconut flavour in Campeltown's renowned Springbank whisky?

Farther south, barley for malting was cultivated until the 1920s, but this gradually became less viable. The climate is damper, cooler and less sunny than in some of the more expansive growing areas. In the 1960s, the Taylor family farm, less than a mile from the sea, revived the idea, and has from time to time grown harvests for Springbank. The farm has been identified on the resultant batches of whisky. Donald Taylor took me into the family home and showed me, on the chimney-breast, a painting of the first new field of barley. "My father asked a local artist to paint that. Not everyone would have thought of it. Mind you, the painter wasn't the best of artists. His cows were never very good."

Springbank itself began as a farm, with an illicit distillery, but has been a legal enterprise for a 170-odd years. Owned by the same family throughout, it has cleaved to tradition wherever possible. Peat was cut locally until the 1960s, and there has been talk of reviving that. Even the coal that fired the stills was mined locally until that

The most eccentric selection of whiskies in Scotland is to be found in a shop called Eaglesome, in Campbeltown.

Spirits
Whiskies
NO ADDED COLOUR~SINGLE CASK~NOT CHILL FILTERED
ORIGINAL COLLECTION
OLD RAJ
DRY GIN

There can be an abandoned look, a silence (below), in a maltings, but the grain spread on the floor is working, slowly approaching germination. Its roots could tangle, but they are separated by being raked (right). After a week, the grains will have developed to their optimum point. Further germination will be halted by drying the grains in a kiln. At that point, they have become malt, ready to be infused with water in the mash-tun.

decade. The last Springbank to use both of those materials was bottled 30 years later and can still sometimes be found. Its label, showing a diagrammatic rendition of a still, is a classic in itself.

In 1992, after twenty years' silence, the maltings at Springbank were extensively repaired and put back into use. The distillery now makes all its own malt, and does all its own bottling. No other distillery in Scotland can quite match that. Springbank has two associate enterprises: Cadenhead buys and bottles hard-to-find malts from all over Scotland; and the nearby shop Eaglesome offers several hundred of them. Combining canniness, a single-mindedness strengthened by its isolation, and a reserve bordering on secrecy, Springbank has gone to extraordinary lengths to uphold, deservedly, the notion of Campbeltown as a whisky region in its own right.

To visit the distillery is to step into this consciousness. In a town full of churches, mainly Protestant, it is hidden behind one, on a street called Longrow. Look for the austere building of the Springbank Evangelical Church, sneak down the alley alongside, and a small courtyard filled with casks announces the distillery. The buildings blend agricultural with early Victorian industrial: the outside painted deep red, a pulley wheel to drive the machinery inside; a large, open door leading to more wheels and belts to move the malt, mill it and stir the infusion in a red-painted, cast-iron, open mash-tun; three stills, the biggest heated by direct flame.

The stills are used in three configurations to make different malt whiskies. No other distillery does this. A double-distilled whisky, made from heavily-peated malt, is called Longrow. This is one of the most assertive whiskies made in Scotland. In 1997, the distillery started to produce an unpeated, triple-distilled whisky, called Hazelburn. This will be released in 2006, and is expected to be quite delicate. The famous Springbank, medium-peated, follows a distilling regime that combines both elements, and is one of the most complex of all malts.

Longrow was a distillery in its own right, one of its warehouses is still used by Springbank Hazelburn was also a distillery, and one of its warehouses remains, on the same street, as offices for a "business park". Connoisseurs of whisky architecture know that small, barred windows suggest a warehouse. It is tempting to believe that every building in Campbeltown fits the bill. Part of the warehousing of the Lochend distillery still stands. The former Benmore distillery's pagoda tower now tops a bus garage. Fragments or built-over sites of about twenty distilleries have been identified.

Springbank also looks after the Glen Scotia distillery on behalf of its owners, Loch Lomond. This distillery is in working order, but has operated sporadically in recent years. It is in an imposing pebbledash building, with dormer-like grain lofts, on a residential street closer to Campbeltown Loch. Whisky-lovers hope that its characteristically briny whisky will not disappear. There is no shortage of ghosts with which to consort in Campbeltown, but the town needs the water of life, too.

The greenest part of Islay, the north of the island, faces Jura. Even this narrow sound can have dangerous seas but, on a calm day, no whisky-lover would visit the one island without going to the other. To miss Jura's distillery would be a singular omission.

ISLAY, THE WHISKIEST ISLAND

As the ferry approaches the rocky south shore, three great Gaelic names declaim their presence: Ardbeg, Lagavulin, Laphroaig. They rise from the water's edge to the rooftops. On a bright day, the sun highlights the stark black type painted on the whitewashed outer walls of each of these famous distilleries. On a stormy day, the tides hurl not only salt but also seaweed against the walls. The atomized spray of brine and iodine fills the atmosphere, permeates the earth and occupies much of the territory, penetrating most powerfully here in the south, where the land quickly rises into a plateau of peat bog. The island once produced salt commercially by dehydration, but that was never its great gift to the world. Not naked salt.

Islay – variously pronounced *ee-luh* (by Gaelic speakers), *eye-luh* (by most Scots) and occasionally *eye-lay* – is by far the greatest whisky island. It is only 25 miles (40 km) long and 15 miles (24 km) wide, with fewer than 4,000 inhabitants, but it has six operating distilleries, a seventh in working order, an eighth that survives only in the bottle, and fragments of more. Yet another distillery is on the adjoining island of Jura.

Two of the distilleries have their own small maltings, burning the local peat. A third, much larger, freestanding maltings uses the same fuel, and to varying extents provides a supply or supplement to every distillery on the island. The three maltings dig from three different peat bogs on the island, each imparting a slightly different taste to the whisky.

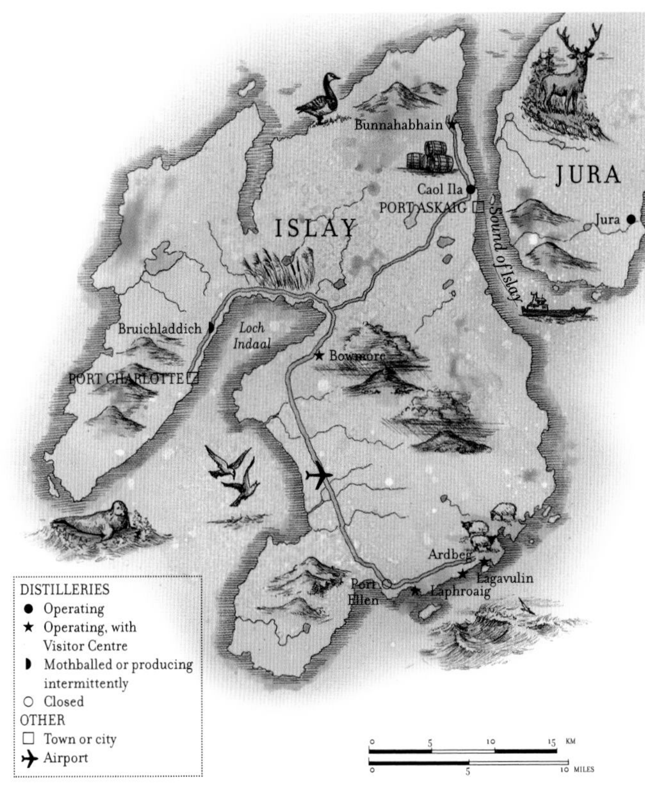

Scotland has two-thirds of the bogland in Britain. The peat's principal component is sphagnum moss, but it includes a rich diversity of other plants and it has been forming for up to 10,000 years. In the Western Isles, especially Islay, the peat is rich in bog myrtle (*Myrica gale*), which has a sweet, cypress-like aroma and bitter flavour. Bog myrtle was one of the flavourings used in beer before the hop plant was adopted, and clearly influences the aroma of the island's peat and whisky.

No other island has more than two distilleries (and only Orkney has two, one making its own peated malt). Islay thus has far more whiskies than any other island. Moreover these include the majority of Scotland's most intense-tasting malts. Other coasts and islands have salty whiskies, other moorlands and mountains offer peat. Islay combines the two with unsurpassed weight, then exceeds either with a further element – the island's coat of seaweed, with its vegetal, medicinal aromas and flavours. Few drinks anywhere in the world have flavours as distinctive as a salty-peaty Islay malt, but the seaweed clinches it.

The island's weather and topography perfect the hydrological cycle, creating a natural system for the production of whisky. As the sea offers up its vapours, the rains immediately find summits of 500 metres (1,640 ft), then seep through quartzite rock in the east, limestone in the north, slate in the middle of the island and ironstone in the west. Whatever mineral flavours are acquired on this trajectory, and as the waters gush from springs, are then overlaid as the resultant streams wash over the peat bogs. This peaty, salty, seaweedy water first influences the whisky when it is used to steep the grains as part of the malting procedure. The peat itself later exerts a second influence when it is employed as fuel to kiln the malt. When this is happening, each of the Islay maltings being on the coast, the smoke of the burning peat and the kilning barley blends with the sea air. The atmosphere is filled with yet more aromas, as though anchovy paste had been spread thickly on freshly-toasted, grainy, thick-cut brown bread. More of the island water adds to the alchemy of earth, wind and fire when it is mixed with the malt in the infusion mash. Finally, the casks of whisky breathe the smoky, peaty, seaweedy, briny atmosphere as they sleep in those coastal warehouses.

All of the working distilleries are at the water's edge. The three mentioned are the most exposed to the sea. One spring day, Ardbeg opened a reception centre for visitors. The following Christmas, the place looked as if it had been shelled. The walls had been penetrated by flying tiles; the rooftop of a malt barn opposite had been swept off by the

The westerly winds blow in from the Atlantic, bouncing off Northern Ireland, and whip the sea into breakers (above). No shelter here. Even on a mild day, they hurl spray on to the island of Islay (opposite). The salty, seaweedy atmosphere pervades much of the island, laying the foundation for its whiskies.

wind. Anyone who lives in an easily-described place wearies of its stereotype, but the people of Islay should not complain too hard about "storm-tossed island".

The island's name may derive from Ella, the daughter of a Scandinavian ruler. From about 800CE, the Vikings raided Islay. It was a prized island. With better soil than other Hebridean islands, it once grew barley on a small scale, although that is no longer economic. There was also some mineral wealth (lime, lead, silver, gold), but any residue is today too costly to work. In the 1300s, Islay was the seat of a domain stretching at times from the Isle of Man and Northern Ireland to Orkney and beyond. This Lordship of the Isles, the original power base of the Clan Macdonald, was one of the eventual components of the Kingdom of Scotland. When the Lords of the Isles set out to defend their domain, they did so from a stone sea-gate that is now part of the site of the Lagavulin distillery.

Each less than a mile from the next, Ardbeg, Lagavulin and Laphroaig are in coves that, from the road, can hide even a modern distillery. Seeing Ardbeg peeking from the rocks, it is easy to imagine illicit distilleries on these sites long before the beginnings of "official" whisky-making in the 1700s. When England and Scotland formed their Union of 1707, laws concerning duties on spirits did not include Islay or the island of Jura. Duties there were in the hands of the Macdonalds' deadly rivals and governors of the islands, the Cawdor Campbells.

Every Islay distillery is by the sea, each with its own jetty, but these landings are too small for commercial use. Today grain is brought in, and whisky shipped out, mainly through Port Ellen.

During the Campbell period, planned villages were built, and they still distinguish Islay from other Hebridean islands. Later, the island was bought by the Morrison family, subsequently the owners of the Bowmore distillery. Their Margadale estate is today the biggest landowner.

The whiskies with the most assertively Islay flavours are produced by that Gaelic triptych: Ardbeg ("small headland"), Lagavulin (pronounced *lag'a'voolin*, with a fairly equal stress on each syllable and meaning "hollow where the grain mill is"), and Laphroaig (pronounced *lafroyg*, and verbosely translated as "beautiful hollow by the broad bay"). Each is almost a hamlet, and the Laphroaig distillery has a room that serves as a village hall, in which weddings can be conducted.

When Ardbeg operated its own maltings, which had no fans to disperse the smoke, that unusual design made for an especially tar-like, oily result. The maltings last operated in 1976–77, and whiskies distilled since then have been less overtly oily, revealing more lemony, applewood flavours, probably imparted by the design of the stills. Despite that compensation, whisky-lovers hope that the maltings may eventually be restored.

The loss of oiliness is a matter of degree: Ardbeg still has the earthiest water supply, originating from two exposed lochs on a nearby hillside. I once rescued a sheep

When even the skies are stormy, the iridescence of the clouds half-hides the pagodas of Ardbeg. This magical headland casts a spell. Around the bay are irises, lilies and a curious scent of saffron. Lovers of Ardbeg become besotted.

The River Kilbride, the water source for the Ardbeg distillery, looks fast enough, and picks up earthy flavours as it flows south. Nearby Lagavulin's water source is peatier, and seems to create a drier, more cutting edge in the whisky.

from one of those lochs, and I still fancy I taste wool in the whisky – the human sense of taste is very suggestible.

When the making of whisky was nothing more than an offspring of local agriculture, the distinctive flavours of the Islay distillates were taken for granted. At the height of the British empire when Scottish soldiers, engineers, teachers and administrators were spreading their national drink around the world, a dash of Islay malt whisky was regarded as an essential element in even the highest-volume blend, and it retained this role for decades. In the heyday of blended Scotches, Ardbeg's most important job was to add its distinctive flavour to the otherwise gentle Ballantine's blends. Lagavulin's water is faster flowing, picking up plenty of peat. The whisky has a crisp, dry peatiness as much as a smokiness. These crisp characteristics give an extra kick to the White Horse blend, and quicken the step of Johnnie Walker. Laphroaig, which has the most fibrous peat, produces the most seaweedy, iodine-like and medicinal whisky. It has added complexity to Long John, among others.

Islay's problem was that, as many blended Scotches became blander in search of wider acceptance, the dash of its whisky fell to 1 per cent or less. Islay became run-down in the 1970s and 1980s, but the growing appreciation of its whiskies as single malts began to have a marked influence in the late 1990s, also bringing whisky tourists to augment the walkers, climbers and birdwatchers. (In winter Islay is inundated with more than 20,000 barnacle geese – supplemented by about 10,000 white-fronted geese. There is also good birdwatching at other times of year, as there are never fewer than 100 species on the island. About that number breed here, and the total bird list runs to 250 species. Rare birds on the island include the corncrake and the chough.)

As the fortunes of Islay improved, the owners of its distilleries came to appreciate their products more. Ardbeg found new proprietors, who invested heavily in restoring production and feeding visitors. Lagavulin's single malt became the bestseller in its owners' Classic Malts range. Laphroaig also became the star performer in its company's range.

As the ferry turns into the harbour, Port Ellen, another vessel may be discharging barley from the mainland, or loading with whisky. The freestanding Port Ellen maltings issues clouds of peat smoke. The colours of the sky filter through reddish-brown, as though the heavens had been tidying autumn leaves into bonfires. The Port Ellen distillery's leafy, herbal, fragrant whisky was always a connoisseurs' choice rather than a fashionable dram. The whisky can still be found, but none has been made for a couple of decades, and the stills have gone.

The little town of Port Ellen became run-down, but it is now restoring its hotels and shops. In 2000, the May festival of local music, which had always included a whisky-nosing competition in the village hall, was extended to include, throughout the island, events devoted to Islay's most famous product. There were still the Gaelic songs and the curiously gabbled mouth-music, but now visitors could compete in the cutting of peat or rolling or bunging of casks; the Lagavulin distillery set up picnic tables and served its whisky with local scallops; the Port Ellen maltings barbecued venison sausage in peaty fireboxes beneath the kilns.

North of Port Ellen, the road runs on over a broad carpet of peat, with only the occasional cottage or agricultural building. The black top bounces slightly, as though there were underlay beneath. The surface moves ahead with a slight ripple. To the east, the peat bogs spread toward the modest mountains. Occasionally, a rabbit scurries across. A mile to the west, a long beach is visible parallel to the road. Some 5 miles (8 km) down the road is a tiny airport, accommodating two scheduled flights a day to and from Glasgow. It has the social ambience of a village bus stop. The airport shop, a single counter, sells home-baked cake with cups of tea.

On the boxy 30-seater there is usually a scatter of passengers from the whisky business. Once, when we almost overshot the runway, I raised an eyebrow to fellow passenger Jim McEwan, a renowned distiller. "I think Prince Charles was driving," he joked. The prince once landed his own plane on Islay, and narrowly avoided a baptism in the bay.

Jim McEwan is an Ileach (*eelach*), which means that he was born on the island. At one stage he was the only Ileach managing a distillery on the island. All the distilleries are owned by groups, and a conscientious young employee from Islay will find himself being promoted to manager on the mainland, while a counterpart from the Lowlands or Highlands may make the opposite journey.

When it was McEwan's turn to be promoted, a better solution was found. From being manager of the Bowmore Distillery, he became it's worldwide embassador. One day he would be entertaining guests on Islay, the next flying to Italy, India or Illinois to present a tasting. Then in 2001, he became part of a group that reopened the Bruichladdich distillery. His services to Bowmore, Bruichladdich, to Islay whisky in general, and to the island, are a legend among those of us for whom it is a special place. He loves to show visitors the island, taking a walk to the harbour in the moonlight, or searching the shore for mussels or oysters next morning. On one occasion, he pointed out a pile of stones and told me: "That was my ancestors'croft. This is McEwan's Hill." The month was February. The purply peat, alder trees and juniper bushes, winter-worn grass, sheep pasture, rushes and reeds, in the subtlest gradations of natural colours, made an island tweed, flecked with the yellow of whin and the white of snowdrops, and criss-crossed with blueish rivulets. Here, the fabric of the island was wet to the touch. Wherever there was the tiniest escarpment or cut in the peaty soil, the water spurted as though from a cloth. The water had gradually flooded even the rockiest farm tracks.

Seeking footholds with some care, we followed the

The painted names identify the distilleries from the sea. On a stormy day high seas will crash against the warehouses, impregnating the earth floors with briny, seaweedy aromas. Behind the distillery the land rises quickly, returning the snow and rain. There can be deluges on both sides.

LAGAVULIN

narrow River Laggan as it rushed over mossy stones and roused its peaty bed. In its final 8 miles (13 km) it enters a narrow canal, dug in 1775 and improved in 1824, to feed the Bowmore distillery. When the malt has been steeped and partially germinated, it is dried over the distillery's slightly sandy peat. Perhaps the sandiness adds a certain dryness and firmness to the whisky. The peat is crumbled before being used, imparting a more smoky fragrance and a less burnt flavour. The distillery is directly exposed to the westerly winds, which help to create a distinct sea-air character in the whisky.

In the middle of the island, the church of Bowmore overlooks the village, which slopes down toward the distillery. It, in turn, overlooks the harbour, on an inlet called Loch Indaal, around which the island bends.

The church is of an unusual circular design, with the intention that the Devil might not hide in corners. Its construction, and that of the village, dates from the 1760s.

The River Laggan (below) flows west, lazily in parts, through reeds and ferns, on its way to Bowmore. The whisky has ferny, lavender-like flavours. The distillery itself overlooks Loch Indaal (opposite), the sea loch that almost bisects the island.

With its central position, Bowmore is regarded as the "capital" of Islay, and a good base for visitors. It is a handsome, well-maintained village, with the busy, successful distillery as its focal point. So important is whisky to the town that Bowmore's school was recently rebuilt with decorative pagodas like those on the vents of the maltings.

Bowmore is the most-visited distillery on the island, in some years attracting as many as 10,000 guests. On one occasion when I called, a schoolteacher visitor had just arrived in his 30-foot (10-metre) sailing boat from Brittany. In McEwan's office, he was being entertained to home-baked fruit loaf and gingerbread. "Look at that butter!" enthused McEwan, adding a little more. The Scottish diet is not for the sedentary.

All of the distilleries have their own little jetties or piers, originally for the importation of barley and the export of finished whisky. Just visible across the loch is the pier at the Bruichladdich distillery. This is separated from the distillery by the coastal road. Bruichladdich, (pronounced *brook laddie*) refers to a banking on the seashore. Even that slight detachment from the sea probably contributes to Bruichladdich being a less salty whisky, and its distinct passionfruit flavour may derive from the ironstone of its water source. This château-like distillery has not worked full-time for six or seven years. It still has

This tiny lade was originally dug more than 200 years ago to channel the river to Bowmore – a mark, both physically and metaphorically, of the very early planning and industrialization that help distinguish Islay from other Hebridean islands. As it flows through the peat, it becomes visibly oily.

The maltings at Bowmore (opposite). The peat fire that dries the malt causes a shower of sparks (bottom left). The peat smoke rises through a sieve-like floor, spread with malt (top). To walk inside the kiln is to contend with a fog of pungent smoke. After the peated malt has been infused in water, the smoky wort is fermented and the resultant "wash" distilled. The stills at Bowmore (bottom right) create whisky of satiny smoothness.

whisky maturing, including some in a surviving warehouse of the Lochindaal distillery, about 3 miles (5 km) down the road in the pretty village of Port Charlotte. Lochindaal ceased distilling in 1929. It was the most westerly distillery in Scotland. Now, Bruichladdich is. When the distillery reopened in 2001, entire families lined the shore outside to hear the speeches. Children were hoisted on to their fathers' shoulders so that, as adults, they could claim to have seen the gates wing open. Those of us who were already adults, allegedly seasoned by the ups and downs of life, found our emotions overflowing. The celebrations lasted all day: a barbecue through the afternoon, a ceilidh in the evening, and fireworks at midnight. Bruichladdich has since added to its range a peatier whisky called Port Charlotte and an even more intense one called Octomore. Neither will be ready for some years. Islay has whisky, tourism, agriculture and fishing, but no major employers. In other densely distilleried regions, a downturn in whisky can send people a few miles farther down the road to work in some other industry; if that happens on Islay, it might mean uprooting. Isolation creates a sense of community in other ways, too. Threatened by the weather, and at the mercy of sea crossings for supplies and for services such as hospital treatment, the islanders understand the meaning of being in the same boat.

At the most remote, westerly point of the island, near Portnahaven seals' shelter, I clambered on the rocks with McEwan to witness what he termed "the power of Islay whisky". It was really the power of the moon and the tides, hurling breakers 20 or 30 feet high on a calm, mild day. I was not sure whether my face was burning or freezing. My lips seemed frozen although I had not touched whisky. Hours later, when my lips were awake, I absent-mindedly licked them and was shocked by the sting of salt.

My visits to the more northerly parts of the island seem to have been on more summery days. Near the tiny northern "town" of Port Askaig is the distillery of Caol Ila, set into a steep hillside dense with fuschias, foxgloves, wild roses and rhododendrons. The name translates as the "Kyle" or "Sound" of Islay, as in a narrow stretch of water. This particular stretch separates Islay from the smaller island of Jura. The Caol Ila distillery dates from 1846, but was extensively modernized in the 1970s. Its whisky is oily, olivey and junipery, perhaps owing something to the limestone water.

A few miles north, the Bunnahabhain distillery produces a fresh, salty, grassy, nutty whisky that is the lightest-tasting of the Islay malts. The name *boona-hav'n* means "mouth of the river", although the waterway is little more than a stream. The distillery actually takes its water from a spring, and is the only one on Islay to do so. It is the most remote of the Islay distilleries, and one of

This ocean-going trawler has lain off the coast near Bunnahabhain since 1974. There have been 250 recorded wrecks or strandings around Islay.

those that built its own hamlet of cottages for its staff. Although whisky-making has changed little, minor mechanizations and efficiencies have freed some of these cottages, which are now rented to vacationers.

From Port Askaig, a ferry that is little more than a motorized platform shuttles to Jura. The crossing is less than a mile. Passengers include children coming to school in Islay, and returning home to Jura. This smaller island, 34 miles (55 km) long but only 8 miles (13 km) wide at its broadest point, takes its name from *dyrer*, a Norse word for deer, which outnumber people. It has about 200 human inhabitants. Among past residents its most famous was George Orwell, who went there to find a peaceful place in which to write the novel *1984*. His hideaway was at the end of the island's one road. The island is noted for mountain peaks known as the Paps (breasts). From the mountains, the very soft water flows down over densely wooded hillsides carpeted with bluebells, pimpernels and wild garlic. The island's whisky is light and piny. The distillery traces its history to 1810, but most of its present buildings are from the 1950s, '60s and '70s.

Opposite the distillery is a tea room and gift-shop. I was amused by a notice I once saw outside: "Anyone who arrives on the island after the shop has closed, please phone Jura 372 for supplies (excluding alcohol)."

This warehouse (below, left) at Caol Ila dates from the 1800s, but the still house was rebuilt in the 1970s. The Paps of Jura (below, right) seem to represent part of the figure of a reclining woman, perhaps a Scottish siren, luring ferry passengers to the island's deceptively mild-tasting whisky and famous cauldron-like tides.

TO MULL

The commuters arriving each morning at the elegantly-arched, marble-floored Queen Street station, in Glasgow, are too sleepily programmed to notice the travellers going the "wrong" way. Or perhaps they are irritated by the Therouvian smugness on the faces of the departing. With only half a dozen carriages, theirs also looks like a commuter train, but the odd fishing line creates suspicions that things might be otherwise.

The train is scarcely out of the station when a pile of casks near the track signals the Glasgow premises of Morrison Bowmore, where Lowland, maritime and Highland malts are bottled: a whiff of the journey ahead. Momentum has increased by Bowling, so whisky-lovers can scarcely glimpse the buildings that survive at the silent Littlemill distillery, on either side of the track. The driver decelerates toward Dumbarton East, and even those odd souls indifferent to whisky are engaged to see the geese that famously guard the warehouses of Ballantine there. The train slows to a halt at Dumbarton Central, affording a view of the brick fortress of Ballantine's grain distillery, and perhaps a container ship loaded with whisky, nosing its way out of the Clyde.

After that, less than half an hour into the journey, it is all steely-blue lochs: Gare, Long, Lomond. They carve their way between hills, crags, and eventually mountains. There is a glimpse of the aptly-named (or so it looks in English) Loch Awe for passengers on the three-hour route to Oban. On the more northerly fork, there will be feats of construction like the astonishing curve at Bridge of Orchy and the precariously tall pagodas of the silent Glenlochy Distillery, at Fort William. There will also be Britain's highest mountain, Ben Nevis. Its year-round snow provides waters for the Ben Nevis distillery, whose manager, Colin Ross, enjoys the paradox that it is also partly maritime, being on a sea loch. The train rounds the northern extreme of the loch

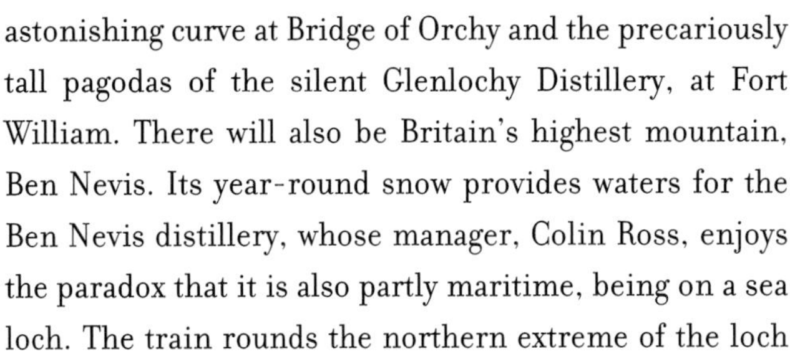

The Sound of Mull (left) can appear to be inconsequentially narrow, but it defines an island, another world. The shimmer of the misty clouds illuminates the grassy hills. The light can be magical on Mull. Rocky outcrops are a reminder of the haunting geology of Mull and its adjoining islands. The land is peatier and boggier (above) where the water flows to the Tobermory distillery. Rocky outcrops are a reminder of the haunting geology of Mull and its adjoining islands. The land is peatier and boggier (above) where water flows to the Tobermory distillery.

and, after five hours, reaches Mallaig. This railway, the West Highland Line, is the iron "Road to the Isles". From Oban, the ferry goes to Mull (whence journeys can be made to nearby Iona and Staffa). From Mallaig, it sails to Skye (although there is now, less romantically, a road bridge across from Kyle of Lochalsh).

Oban is the the capital of the Western Highlands, its Victorian architecture (notably a folly modelled on Rome's Colosseum) recalling its heyday. In the late 1700s and the 1800s, it was the "Gateway to the Isles", during the Romantic movement and the steamship and railway eras.

The story of habitation in the Western Highlands gained a new chapter when remains of cave-dwellers from the Mesolithic era were found at the Oban distillery. The distillery itself dates from the 1790s, and the relics were found 100 years later, when a cliff was being excavated to make room for new warehouses. On the same part of the site, what looked like a hook for boats suggested that the sea might once have bitten further in the bay. Oban's whiskies have a distinct West Highlands brininess – very much a whiff of the sea. The distillery overlooks the bay, not far from the ferry. At one stage, the Oban whisky also contributed to a blend called Old Mull.

St Columba encouraged the planting of barley, and his rules for monastic life included the need to brew. In the year 563CE, he established on the island of Iona an abbey that would become influential throughout Europe. Remnants of what has been described as "a brewery or bakery" have been found during restoration work. Parts of today's abbey date from the 1200s, more from the 1400s, and the whole was extensively restored in the early 1900s. It is today occupied by an ecumenical Christian community. In the cloister, a carving shows someone drinking from a goblet – but perhaps receiving the sacrament rather than enjoying a beer or whisky. In the centre of the cloister, a modern sculpture called "The Descent of the Spirit" (Jacob Liebschitz, 1966) has an altogether more metaphorical meaning. In the village shop, it is possible to buy a bothy blanket (the word means "hut", but often indicates an illicit distillery) or a quaich (drinking vessel), but most visitors are attracted by the island's religious history, or in the hope of seeing puffins.

The island, which has a human population of about a hundred, is only 3½ miles (5.5 km) long, 1½ miles (2.5 km) wide, a ridge of rock, most of it clothed in pasture. The ferry takes five or ten minutes from the hamlet of Fionnphort, on Mull.

Fionnphort is also the starting point for the tour boats to the uninhabited rocky islet of Staffa. This journey takes 45 minutes to an hour, subject to the weather. Even on a calm day, the prevailing westerly winds can create quite a swell.

Iona, a rocky foothold of civilization after the Dark Ages. The cultivation of barley was a beginning, but not easy here. Island communities struggle to survive, and thank God when they do. The abbey (opposite, above) and its chapel (right) have a simple beauty. The cloister (left) is only slightly more ornamental.

Clinging for dear life: a precarious-looking handrail waits to guide visitors to the mouth of Fingal's Cave (left). The columns that fringe the entrance (above) look man-made, but they were created by far greater forces. Did giants once walk here, and bring the metaphysical process of distillation?

"That's what gives you the music in Fingal's Cave," explained boatman David Kirkpatrick. I asked him about a similar phenomenon on Mull: the illusion of pipe music on Calgary Beach. "I don't know about that. North Mull is a foreign country to me," he observed. At the time, we were a good 10 miles (16 km) from Calgary Beach. The boatman's Scottish reserve evaporated whenever wildlife appeared. He clearly enjoyed spotting seals on the sheer rocks that make this sea a maze; shags nesting in caves,

shearwaters skimming the waves. Not only are the seas here dangerous, there is also a lack of safe anchorages. That has threatened at times to depopulate the islands.

Defying the growing swell, Kirkpatrick stood in the helm of his 45-foot (14-metre) motorboat and somehow persuaded it to lie alongside the half-dozen concrete steps that serve as a landing stage for Staffa. He has been doing this since he was a boy, but some days he can still be beaten by the weather. The steps are built into a rock formation that could belong to another planet. The island seems to comprise entirely columns of basalt, so dark and smooth that they could be made of tar, coal or Bakelite. A cable "bannister" has been hooked to the columns to enable visitors to climb to the entrance of Fingal's Cave. This cavern, 60 ft (18 m) high and more than 200 ft (61 m) deep, is like a natural cathedral, with the columns as organ pipes. The seawater floor is the colour of marble; the descending columns hint at gargoyles; the reflections on the lichen-tinged walls suggest stained glass. The curiously sweet saltiness in the air could be incense. This

One of Scotland's prettiest harbours, Tobermory shows its colours as a yacht anchorage. Its pastel waterfront also embraces the island's distillery. The town was largely built in 1788.

is a malt moment: unhook the hip flask of Tobermory or Ledaig. Some suggest a personal stereo and the Hebrides Overture, but electronics seem hardly appropriate, or necessary. As the waves ebb and flow, Mendelssohn's motif echoes in the mind. The composer was perhaps led to this remote location by the writing of Sir Walter Scott. The novelist may in turn have been inspired by James Macpherson's epic poem *Fingal*, allegedly translated from an ancient Gaelic manuscript. Perhaps the hero Fingal (*Fion na Gael*) was the giant who brought the art of distillation across the rocky "causeway" from Ireland ... .

After I had breathed the air of early Christianity and Celtic myth, the journey back was slow. It was not just the two hours' drive from Fionnphort to Tobermory, the main town of Mull, but also the otherworldiness of the landscape. The first stretch follows the shore, rocky with pink granite. Then the scenery changes as the road passes through a deep glen with three or four peaks at either side. That day, the peaks looked as though they were emitting white smoke. Then the sun would brighten, and the clouds would forge themselves into shimmery gold, slicing the hilltops. Or evaporate again and hang like a mist in the glen. From the hills, narrow waterfalls plunged hundreds of feet. Between the sun's beams, rain in a fine spray had blown the grass in two directions, each reflecting a different shade of green, resembling a cloth of worn velvet.

Tobermory is entered by a steep, winding road. Above the town is a cairn recalling the meaning of its name: St Mary's Well. The original water source was said to be a reason for the settlement. The monument, built in 1902 for the coronation of King Edward VII, embraces a fountain. Unfortunately, someone has removed the tap. Higher still, the Tobermory distillery takes its water from a small, unnamed loch in a stretch of peaty land, dense with bog myrtle, bracken and heather and fringed with Corsican pines and larch.

At the foot of the road, the distillery itself is tucked into the hillside. It has great charm. The distillery dates from 1798 and, even by the standards of the industry, has a chequered history, but it has enjoyed a new lease of life since it was acquired by the blenders Burn Stewart. The copper dome of the mash-tun shines anew. Mashman Stuart O'Donnell has painted a mural in the tun-room, which has a new, open-beam ceiling made from retired washbacks. The two sets of stills, with curiously stepped, rising, lyne arms shine behind a window that might suit a small church. One set of stills makes an unpeated whisky, under the Tobermory name. The other has seen the welcome return of a peated malt called Ledaig (sometimes pronounced *lechig*; it means "safe haven"). Even the "plain" version has a hint of peat, from the water. The Ledaig has a smoky sweetness. Unfortunately, neither is likely to have a great deal of maritime character. The previous owner sold the impressive, four-storey warehouse as apartments. The whisky is now aged on the mainland. At the distillery, the visitor centre is the former Tobermory fire station. Now it extinguishes thirst.

One of Scotland's greatest and most intense-tasting whiskies – Talisker – is distilled on a seaweedy inlet on Skye. Its flavours are as dramatic as the Cuillin Hills behind.

TO SKYE

Even today, Mallaig has the sense of a frontier town. One expects a whaler or factory ship to dock by the Mallaig Ice Company and defectors in fur hats to occupy the Seamen's Mission. In a crowded bar there one night, I watched a band comprising an accordionist and two spoon-players, rendering ever more furious reels. The accordionist urged patrons, with an insistence that verged on threat, to dance. A couple reluctantly complied, danced out of the front door, and were never seen again.

The romance of the ferry timetable is a music sheet in a minor key. Its first offering from Mallaig is headed "Small Isles", as though other options might be Medium, Family-size or Giant. Like some other small countries, Scotland feels an affection toward the diminutive. The Small Isles is the proper name given to Eigg, Muck, Rum and Canna, all lying just to the south of Skye.

This was a frontier for Neolithic agriculturists, around 4,000 years ago. Shards of pottery from that period, found in an archaeological dig on the island of Rum in 1987, appeared to have contained a fermented drink made from barley, oats, honey, heather, meadowsweet and various herbs – a conclusion based on the established technique of analyzing pollen and spores found in encrustations on the pottery. The analysis was carried out by an archaeo-botanist, with some technical and financial assistance from Glenfiddich. The company also attempted to recreate the brew, which emerged as a thin, winey, sweet, pale drink. The island is owned by Scottish Natural Heritage, and has a population of 39. It is managed as a nature reserve, but has no exhibit or cairn to mark the site of the dig.

Across the water on Skye, the name of Talisker has a more obvious resonance for the whisky-lover. Talisker is said to mean "sloping rock". Several such rocks guard the secluded Talisker Bay, on the western side of the island. Nearby is Talisker House, believed to have been built around 1720, although it has been extended several times

Talisker House is now a small hotel. It is set in 50 acres (20 hectares) of gardens and woods, leading to Talisker Bay.

since. An engraving from 1772 shows women grinding barley at Talisker House. It was for several generations home to the local lairds of the Clan MacLeod. During that time it was visited by the English lexicographer Samuel Johnson, whose 1755 dictionary offered the first citation of the word "whisky". Johnson, characteristically grumpy about the Scots, found Talisker bleak. His companion and biographer James Boswell, a Scot, admired the garden, which remains impressive. Today, Talisker House is a small hotel, with four guest bedrooms.

It was at one stage the home of the MacAskill family, who farmed the estate and in 1830 built the Talisker distillery, across Hawk Hill at Carbost, on a natural harbour near the head of Loch Harport. An early admirer of the whisky was Robert Louis Stevenson, who in 1880 said that the king of drinks was one of these three: Talisker, Islay whisky or The Glenlivet. As well as being a writer and educated in law, Stevenson was an engineer (his family's practice worked on lighthouses in the Western Isles). Perhaps his legal mind felt that Talisker should be placed in a category of its own. Or was his interest in engineering engaged by an island distillery with three stills?

While the most robust of the Islay malts have the most evident maritime character, Talisker and Highland Park (from Orkney) are today by far the most assertive from other islands. Admirers of Talisker often attribute its distinctively peppery character to the Cuillin: a ridge of volcanic mountains and their lava flows. The whisky has been said to be "the lava of the Cuillins" and "to explode on the palate". Part of the ridge, dominated by dark rock called gabbro, is known as Black Cuillin. A granite segment, paler in colour, is dubbed Red Cuillin. The distillery is about 6 miles (9.5 km) from the peaks, but these mountains dominate the island and are its symbol. There was an outcry in the year 2000 when the clan chief of the MacLeods announced that he might have to sell a part of the range to finance repairs to Dunvegan Castle, his home in the north of the island. The Cuillins offer the longest and most challenging ridge walk in the British Isles.

There are several possible explanations for the name Cuillin but the most commonly accepted origin is the Norse word for the keel of a boat. Perhaps the ridge reminded the Vikings of an upturned longboat. That image has its own drama but hardly equals the massive intrusion of molten rock from deep below the Earth's crust that began this freak landscape. Lovers of Skye often talk of the "power" of the Cuillins. The metaphor is apt. The gabbro and granite of the mountains give way at lower altitudes to outcrops of softer, orange-red strata. Touch this rock and it leaves a chalky dust on the finger.

This stone can be found near the distillery, and I feel sure it explains the "lava" taste. The distillery insists that Talisker's water rises from granite, and is low in mineral

Talisker means "Sloping Rock" ... but which one? Two candidates guard the bay, and there are others. Gaelic names often describe the landscape of a location. In translation, they can sound similar to Native North American names.

content, although with some peat character. The water is collected from springs on Hawk Hill, home to several birds of prey, including peregrines. The distillery's literature talks of fourteen springs being in use, although more are available. The water for mashing is piped, while that for cooling is collected from a burn that passes through the distillery grounds. Medium-peated malt is employed. Talisker's current owners, United Distillers, have in recent years promoted the argument that the shape of the stills is the key element in determining

flavour. While this factor is increasingly appreciated, it is only one of several influences. Talisker switched to double-distillation in 1928, but its wash stills are of an unusual design. They have an unusually slender boil-ball (the swelling in the neck that can cause vapours to fall back in "reflux"). More significantly, there is a "reflux pipe" that recirculates some of the vapours. This might be expected to create a lighter spirit, but stills do not always deliver what is predicted. They have a life of their own. A lemon-skin, applewood fruitiness is imparted by a similar device at Ardbeg, but that is part of the spirit still. Perhaps Talisker's stills add a slight sourness? They are also unusual in that the lyne arm forms an inverted horseshoe before entering a traditional worm tub (the coil in which the vapour is then condensed). Together, all of these peculiarities must add complexity. So must the location. The smartly-kept, whitewashed distillery is at the foot of a steep hill and on a sheltered part of a somewhat remote loch. It is a sea loch, and seaweed is much in evidence around the mouth of the distillery's burn. There was once a kelp industry in the area. Scotland is especially rich in seaweed, mainly Laminarian kelp, and the densest "forests" are around Skye.

Opposite the distillery, almost falling into the loch, is a pub with bedrooms. Enjoying a Talisker in its low-ceilinged public bar, I noticed on the wall a chart with illustrations of the loch's flora and fauna. Three types of seaweed were shown, along with thrift (also known as the sea pink), a form of sea lavender. The chart had been designed by the pupils of Carbost Primary School.

The clouds above Skye can seem high and bright, evoking thoughts of the Norsemen's Valhalla.

Could there one day be a second distillery, at the south end of the island? As Talisker becomes ever more popular in the Classic Malts range, it is likely to be less available to blenders of the various other products that associate themselves with Skye. The whisky liqueur Drambuie, which contains some fine old malts, romantically claims to be based on a drink served to Bonnie Prince Charlie when he was a fugitive on Skye. The blend is made in Edinburgh. A range of perfumy, lightly peaty, dryish blends under the label Isle of Skye is said to have been created by a MacLeod in Skye 100 years ago, but it is now made in East Lothian.

A more distinctive product is a vatted malt called "Poit Dhubh" (*potch dhu*, referring to a "black pot", or illicit still). This is full of earthy, vegetal, spicy flavours. Té Bheag nan Eilean (*chey vek nan yellan*, "The Little Lady of the Isles") is a blend, soothingly oily, with touches of peat. These products were devised by Sir Iain Noble, a former Edinburgh banker who has tried several times to launch ventures that would offer employment on the island. As his whisky names suggest, Sir Iain is also keen to promote the Gaelic language, which some islanders speak. His office is on the Eilean Jarmain estate on Skye. He owns a hotel there, too, and has talked of establishing a distillery on a nearby farm.

TO ORKNEY

"The most famous whisky was an essential ingredient in the bride's cog at a wedding. It wet the lips of new-born babies ... . Ten years after he was dead, a stone jar of his whisky was found. 'Never, never, never was there stuff like it,' said the mason who found it. 'I lived in the Island of the Young, an enchanted man, for three days until that stone jar was dry.'" So wrote George Mackay Brown in *The Troubling of the Waters*.

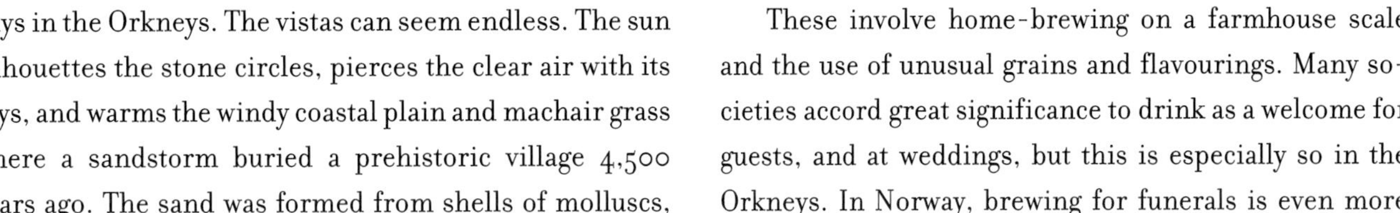

In his later years the Orcadian poet lived in a house on the site of the long-demolished local distillery in the town of Stromness, on the main island.

The Land of the Midnight Sun may be farther north, but there is a similar shimmering beauty to long summer days in the Orkneys. The vistas can seem endless. The sun silhouettes the stone circles, pierces the clear air with its rays, and warms the windy coastal plain and machair grass where a sandstorm buried a prehistoric village 4,500 years ago. The sand was formed from shells of molluscs, and rocks crushed to powder by glaciers. It is almost white. Then, in the short days of midwinter, the Orkneys become the Dark Islands, the moisture glistening in the gently rolling peat moors.

The Orkney islands and their even more northerly neighbours the Shetlands have been part of Scotland since 1470, but were previously under Scandinavian rule for about 700 years.

Even today, Thorfin, Sigurd and Inga are sometimes encountered as forenames. Some of the islands' drinking customs belong to a tradition common to rural communities in Norway and Sweden (notably the island of Gotland) and the distinct cultures of Finland and Estonia.

These involve home-brewing on a farmhouse scale and the use of unusual grains and flavourings. Many societies accord great significance to drink as a welcome for guests, and at weddings, but this is especially so in the Orkneys. In Norway, brewing for funerals is even more

The thinly-populated islands offer endless vistas, with little to resist the wind (opposite); and long journeys to find friends. As winter darkens, the warmth is in the hot punch, with beer, whisky and spices. Buttercups may blossom (above), but trees are few.

important. "It can be windy here, dark and cold in winter, and the islands are thinly populated. People made long journeys to visit friends or relatives, and needed a warming drink when they arrived," an Orcadian explained to me. The "cog" is a vessel filled with a hot punch based on home-brewed beer, whisky, brown sugar and spices. "A wedding without a bridal cog would be unthinkable," the same young woman told me.

The term cog refers to both the vessel and the drink. The vessel, always made from wood, is shaped like a pail, with two upright handles. It is much the same as a vessel used in Scandinavia, and is regarded with even greater symbolism in Finland and Estonia, where it is employed to serve beers made partly from rye and flavoured with juniper. Cog is sometimes pronounced almost like "keg", a word of Scandinavian origin. A similar-sounding word, "quaich" (pronounced *quake*, with a guttural ending), is used throughout Scotland to describe a traditional drinking vessel specifically for whisky. A quaich also has two handles, although they lie flat, and the vessel is bowl-shaped and traditionally silver.

The unusual grain used in Orkney is bere, (pronounced *bare)*. The resemblance to the word "beer" is not a coincidence. Some etymologists believe that a grain from which it was possible to brew was deemed "beer-like", with that expression becoming "barley", both words perhaps rooted in the now-extinct Baltic language Old Prussian. What the islanders call bere is an early form of barley. Similar early barleys were grown elsewhere in Europe, including the northern mainland of Scotland, but bere is a conspicuous survivor in Orkney and Shetland.

It usually has four rows of grain in each ear (as opposed to the more common two- or six-row types of barley usually used to make beer and whisky). There is plenty of well-drained, sweet soil in the Orkneys, and the basins and mounds of the landscape are gentle enough to provide space for cultivation, although also exposed to the winds. Bere's sturdy straw helps it withstand the breezes, and its quick ripening, without a requirement for much sun, suits the short summers. Its disadvantage is that it has a lower yield of fermentable sugars than conventional barleys. For this reason, northern Scottish farmers felt in 1707 that bere should be taxed at a lower rate than English barley, and this debate threatened the signing of the Act of Union between the two countries.

Bere is used to make porridge, a flat bread called the bannock, and in home-brewing. It was employed in distilling, both illicit and legal, probably until after World War I. Although it is no longer employed for this purpose, its continued cultivation is a reminder of a unique distilling tradition on Orkney. Every baker on the islands still makes bere bannocks, which are the size of a pancake and as doughy as a scone – a more generous counterpart of the rye crispbreads of Scandinavia, which are baked in farm buildings also used for brewing. The bannocks, like the crispbreads, are often served with cheese. I was surprised to be told that, until the two World Wars, baker's yeast had not been widely employed in the islands. Domestic ovens had not been usual. Orcadian hunger had been accommodated by bannocks, cooked on girdles, or clootie dumplings, steamed in a pot. One home-brewer told me she believed that yeast for beer had been cultured from moulds on potatoes. This sounds unlikely, but I have seen oranges put to a similar purpose in Mexico.

In all of these uses, bere produces a darker colour and stronger taste than conventional barley. It embodies the sense that a crop sufficiently resilient to survive in a cold and windy climate will both look and taste robust. Its awns are rough, spiny and longer than those on normal barley. I was shown an ear of the grain by Harriet Craigie, the custodian on a smallholding that is operated as a farm museum, on the main island of the Orkneys. (There are about 70 islands, of which around 20 are inhabited. The principal island is known as "the mainland".)

The bere seemed to hook itself to her cardigan and move up her sleeve, as though the grain were alive and seeking to escape with its life. "It just keeps climbing," she said. "Those awns are like fish-hooks." The farm has a kiln, built from stone and reminiscent in shape of a beehive or igloo. The outside is covered in grass. Inside is a hearth and a wire platform on which the grain could rest. It was used both to dry grain prior to milling and in the malting process. I asked, stupidly, if the hearth had burned peat. "We have hardly any trees on the island, so we couldn't burn wood. The nearest coal mines were in Fife. Of course we used peat!" Remoteness is measured not in miles but in accessibility.

Trees are not entirely absent, but they do tend to blow into a wedge shape. Houses in the country are built low, with small windows and doors, as though they are huddling against a gale.

I have seen the power of the wind as it hurled the water against the wheel of Barony Mill, which still grinds bere for domestic use and for bakers and home-brewers. The waters rush by at 110,000 gallons (500,000 litres) an hour, whirring the wheel that drives rumbling beechwood cogs and French quartz millstones. One of the mill's floors can be used for malting, and it has a kiln. Rae Phillips, the third member of his family to run the mill, told me he remembered people bringing their own peat so that they could kiln bere to the taste they preferred.

He offered me a glass of his own home-brew. It tasted dusty and grainy. Not for the first time, perhaps I was being suggestible. There were also drily syrupy, apricot-like notes. These no doubt derived from esters formed in fermentation; he had used yeast bought from a homebrew supply store. Rae used no flavourings other than hops, but some islanders have been known to employ sorrel. Heather Ale is also made in the Orkneys, although it is usually based on sugar rather than grain. Before refrigeration, beer was sometimes buried for storage during summer, a technique also known in northern Germany. A favourite storage place in Orkney was the peat moor.

A local folk hero, with a typically Orcadian-Scandinavian name, Magnus Eunson, was a famous illicit distiller. He was also a church officer, and is reputed to

have hidden his whisky under the pulpit. Eunson is said to have found the perfect water supply near the main town, Kirkwall, and thus inspired the location of the legal Highland Park distillery, in 1798. Even after the legal distillery had been founded, Eunson himself continued to turn the water into whisky.

Highland Park is the most northerly distillery in Scotland, and its whisky is one of the nation's finest. The distillery's best-known source of water is in an area called Green Vale, among farmland, about half a mile to the east. There, springs feed a pond called "Catty Maggie's Quarry". The lady in question was the doyenne of local tinkers, and very fond of felines. She lived near the quarry, which yielded a type of flagstone named after the nearby island of Rousay. Flagstone, a variation of mudstone from the Middle Devonian period (380 million years ago), is the bedrock of Orkney, although red sandstone is often more visible. A blue, fine-grained flagstone known locally as "walliwall" is used in construction, and is very evident in the buldings at Highland Park. This geological base gives rise to hard, carbonate-rich waters and full-flavoured whiskies.

The malt shovel is a symbol of both brewing and distilling (opposite). Like the rake, it is a means of turning the malt, ensuring that the grain remains aerated and cool, and that its rootlets (visible in the inset picture) do not tangle. A maltster shovelling by hand develops a pattern and a rhythm that help to spread the grains evenly across the malting floor. Manual methods add fine-tuning to the work of turning machines.

Catty Maggie's Quarry today is surrounded by irises, and lilies grow in the water. In summer, the air is floral and "green"-smelling. This water, which is quite hard and iron-tinged, is used mainly in steeping at the beginning of the malting process.

In his 1887 classic *The Whisky Distilleries of the United Kingdom*, Alfred Barnard said that Highland Park distilled mainly from bere. Today, conventional barley is used. Highland Park makes about 20 per cent of its own malt, and this is highly significant in the flavour of the whisky.

The water used in mashing usually comes from an underground spring in marshy fields about half a mile west of the distillery. The well-head is so overgrown with dock leaves and nettles that a distillery worker had difficulty finding it to show me. Within these fields several sources have been used over the years. The fields are also bisected by the Crantit Burn, and two ponds gather more water to cool the condensers. A pumping station takes the water uphill to the distillery. The water sources, the distillery, and the island's main town, Kirkwall, are all on a neck of land about a mile and a half wide, between two stretches of water, the Wide Firth and Scapa Flow. It is a doubly maritime location, and very exposed in its hillside position.

A huge influence on the whisky is the local peat, cut from heathland that supports a wide variety of grasses, sedges and maritime plants such as the blue-flowered spring squill and the sea plantain. Orkney peat imparts a distinctly fragrant smokiness. The peat is cut on

The peat on Hobbister Moor is heathery and briny, as it is fringed by the sea. Each of these elements contributes to the flavour of Highland Park whisky. To prevent his hands from blistering, a cutter will often use a tool with a cow-horn handle. The shaft will be oak or teak. Some cutters score the turf in March, before the vegetation grows new roots. Much of the actual cutting is done in May. The cut peat looks like dark chocolate fudge.

Hobbister Moor, about 4 miles west of the distillery. Highland Park owns 1,500 acres (600 hectares) of this swirly moorland, and reckons to have 400 years' supply of peat. Hobbister Moor is also a nature reserve, noted for birds ranging from the fierce Arctic skua to the often gregarious curlew and starling. A peat-cutter told me that a starling had nested in his mechanical digger.

On the moor much of the heather is "burned" white by the salty winds and spray from Scapa Flow. In places it grows horizontally to avoid the wind. Near the cliff edges heather gives way to more salt-tolerant plants, such as red fescue, buck's-horn plantain and thrift.

Barnard talked of the "German Ocean" and the Atlantic creating "a seething cauldron of enraged waters" in the channels between the Scottish mainland and

Orkney. It is said that lamb grazed on Orkney can be eaten with no additional salt. I have not totally persuaded myself that the meat is so obviously salty, but the whiskies certainly are.

Highland Park's saltiness is tempered by the use of some sherry butts, the fragrant peatiness of the malt and the fullness of a spirit from quite fat stills. The result is a superbly rounded, full-flavoured malt.

Less than half a mile south, the Scapa distillery overlooks the waters from which it takes its name. It uses unpeated malt, although a certain oiliness is imparted by a wash-still in the unusual Lomond style, which has a column neck. There are also very slight hints of peat and heather at some ages, presumably picked up from the burn that supplies the water. The whisky is less rich, but has its own complexity, and has a following for its robust saltiness. The distillery was built in 1885, and has a restored water-wheel, but most of today's buildings date from the late 1950s and are somewhat bunker-like. Scapa has operated only sporadically in recent years and has, unaccountably, been neglected by its absentee owners at a time when island whiskies are in the ascendant.

THE EAST

Wilderness, mountain basins, snowmelt, burns and rivers ... the most densely distilleried valley ... and the richest farmland.

The grandeur of the Grampians. Their yawning, stretching, lazy muscularity seems to push apart the craggy West and the more accessible East. Each has its own charm for the traveller.

The sharp-looking stacks are yet another of Scotland's strange rock formations, and the flagstone under Caithness is a likely influence on the local whisky, Old Pulteney. Beyond these northerly extremes, and especially south of Brora, the countryside becomes less wild, and the distilleries more evident.

FROM WICK TO INVERNESS

Rock "stacks", remnants of an earlier coastline eroded by wind and sea, guard the northernmost mainland of Scotland. As the plane makes its final approach, stratified, ochre-and-white cliffs support the land as though the whole thing were a schoolroom model made of clay. These distinctive formations of flagstone lie underneath much of the county of Caithness.

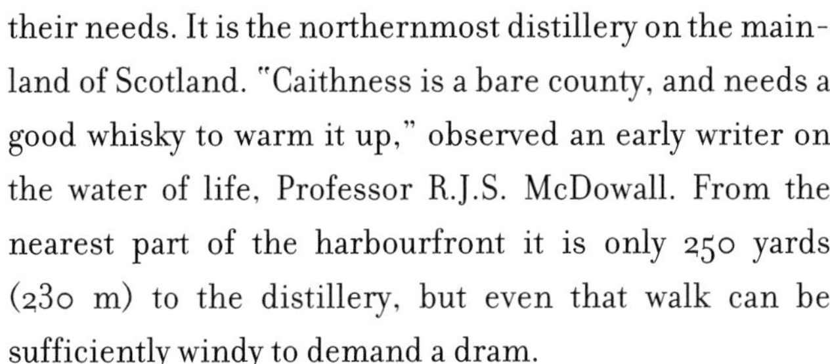

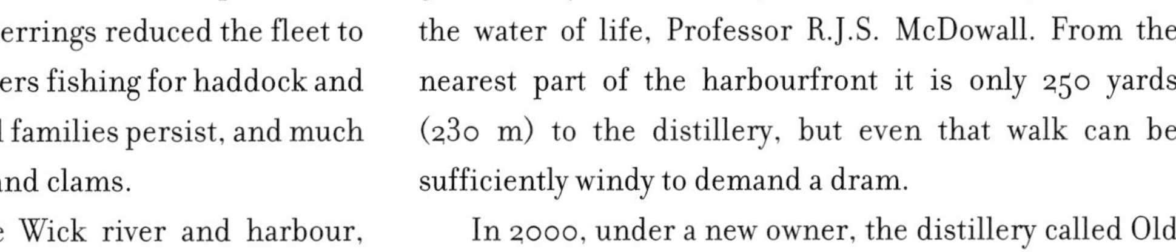

A Norse invader today might light upon the familiarity of Wick, its reductive Viking name initially meaning a bay or creek (and possibly related to the Anglo-Saxon word for "settlement"). Wick was once the north's herring capital, although today its harbour, designed by Thomas Telford, seems unnecessarily elaborate. Where the harbour was once paved with small boats, the depletion of herrings reduced the fleet to single figures, with seine-netters fishing for haddock and whiting. Today, only a few local families persist, and much of the catch is lobsters, crabs and clams.

On the south side of the Wick river and harbour, Telford also designed housing, constructed from local stone, for the fishermen. This area is named after a member of a local family, the Pulteneys, who were prominent in fisheries and politics. Having been built for working men, the houses are small, making for a strangely attenuated version of Georgian elegance and spaciousness. The male residents may have found escape within the local pubs, which were described as "seminaries of Satan" by a local clergyman. He was outraged that fishermen indulged themselves in "enormous potations", but a distillery was nonetheless built in Pulteneytown in 1827 to supply their needs. It is the northernmost distillery on the mainland of Scotland. "Caithness is a bare county, and needs a good whisky to warm it up," observed an early writer on the water of life, Professor R.J.S. McDowall. From the nearest part of the harbourfront it is only 250 yards (230 m) to the distillery, but even that walk can be sufficiently windy to demand a dram.

In 2000, under a new owner, the distillery called Old Pulteney added a visitor centre. This is entered by what

Brora has gently briny breezes ... but its distilleries are a few hundred metres from the seafront. They nonetheless pick up maritime flavours. The saltiness in the whiskies diminishes where the coast is more sheltered.

appears to be an insignificant-looking private house, originally the home of the manager. Set within the door a window has been etched to depict a herring boat. Inside, the corridor that leads to the visitor centre has been tricked out to look like a companion way in a boat. The distillery itself is hidden by very functional warehouses, giving the site an anonymous industrial appearance.

The nutty flavours in the whisky perhaps owe something to water that rises from Caithness stone. Its fruitiness is no doubt influenced by the very oddly-shaped stills. The wash-still has a huge boil-ball (a swelling in the neck), a flat head and a lyne arm that sweeps downward. The spirit still has a lyne arm that bends over double, into a purifier, then rises again. The more salient characteristic is the saltiness of the whisky. For this reason it has long been known as the Manzanilla of the north. Some Old Pulteney is matured in sherry butts, but most sleeps in first-fill Bourbon barrels. The salt is surely in the air.

Inland, Caithness and the adjoining county of Sutherland are damp and peaty. Centred on the hamlet of Forsinard are 1 million acres (400,000 hectares) of reedy marshland, gullying into oily pools between boulder-strewn hummocks. This area, with a richness of unusual bog plants, is regarded as a distinctive ecosystem of global significance: a northern tundra, albeit in a relatively southerly location and climate. The Norse name for such countryside was *flói*, and this Scottish manifestation is known as The Flow Country. The single-track, two-carriage railway through Flow Country looks like a precarious toy. The road is so slender that travellers can forget their own presence and imagine that humankind has abdicated the planet to the greenshank, the black-throated diver and the golden plover. On the coast, there is a lesser illusion, where the main road crosses bridges above straths or glens. Down by the waterside, it is easy to forget the traffic high above. At Dunbeath, the fishing village is still sufficiently detached to evoke the lyrical novel *Highland River*, by Neil Gunn, who was born there. Like Burns, he once supported himself by working as an exciseman, and later paid literary tribute to whisky. He felt that he recognized in Old Pulteney "some of the strong characteristics of the northern temperament".

This stretch of northern coastline has no more distilleries until Clynelish, at the fishing and golfing resort of Brora, an area of clay, sandstone and shale. On the west side of the road, the 1960s distillery stands proudly on a modest hillside, overlooking an ornamental fountain. Hiding behind a thicket of sycamores is its predecessor, the Brora distillery, intact and with pagoda, but now overgrown. Brora whiskies can still be found, and are usually peatier than those from Clynelish. Both are oily and firm, with a mustardy note and a maritime saltiness, and their influence is notable in some of the older Johnnie Walker blends.

The Brora distillery was established very early – in 1819, at a time when new industry in the south and the resultant commerce were changing the economics, politics and social structures of the Highlands. The

distillery's founder, the first Duke of Sutherland, was infamously associated with the Highland Clearances, when aristocrats decided that grazing land for their sheep should take priority over family smallholdings.

Brora, rebuilt in the 1890s, is a classically pretty distillery. There is another example near Edderton (the name meaning "peaty place"), on the south side of the Dornoch Firth. As the distillery of the Balblair Farm, it dates from at least the 1790s, but the present building, on a slightly different site, is from 1895. Even then, the influence of the water supply was appreciated. The farm distillery had used peaty water taken by an open lade from the old, red sandstone, siltstone and mudstone of the Struie Hills. This was piped to the new premises, and still is. A burn that already passed by the site was ignored. In the mash house, I was surprised to see that a fan-tailed dove had taken up residence. This bird had persuaded the distillery cat, a black-and-white tom, of the virtues of peaceful coexistence. The whisky has some sea-breeze fragrance, a textured body, a distinct fruitiness and the faintest hint of peat.

The Brora distillery (above) has not worked for some years, but its whiskies can still be found. The more modern Clynelish is nearby.

The distillery famously associated with water that rises from sandstone is Glenmorangie, just outside Tain. The town itself, dating from 1630, is handsomely built from sandstone. About 875 yards (800 metres) from the distillery is a small pond, in Tarlogie Wood on the edge of the Morangie Forest. On the sandy bed of the pond, tiny holes are formed by water rising from the earth and bubbling toward the surface. The area has been decorated with a bridge and handrails made from larch. The water rises from sandstone and limestone hills in the forest, and imparts a distinct, minerally firmness to the whisky. The Glenmorangie whisky is also shaped by the tallest stills in Scotland, making for a lightness and delicacy. A further influence is the siting of the warehouses, separated from the Firth only by the railway. Some are slightly nearer the water than others, and have vents facing the sea. Sampling in the warehouses, I noted that some offered saltier whiskies than others.

This area is dotted with whiskies. From the train you can see the Invergordon grain distillery spread on either side of the track. Between 1965 and 1977, Invergordon also had a malt distillery called Ben Wyvis. In 2000, I tasted a rare bottling of this whisky. It had a lightly peaty, peppery, passionfruit character. Some years earlier, Invergordon made a distillation from bere, to mark the 500th anniversary of the first reference to distilling in Scotland. I sampled this at the same company's nearby Dalmore distillery, and found it easily drinkable, with

One of the best views of a traditional Scottish distillery is afforded by Balblair, on the Wick–Inverness railway line. The distillery dates from the 1890s, and is little changed in structure.

oily, cereal-grain flavours. Dalmore, at Alness, on the Cromarty Firth, produces a rich, orangey, marmaladey whisky. Its neighbour Teaninich also makes a big-bodied whisky, but one with more of a malt emphasis.

The village of Muir of Ord ("the Moor by the Hill") has a distillery with a sizeable modern maltings – Glen Ord, which makes a malty, fragrant whisky with a whiff of peat. Glen Ord might claim to be geographically the nearest descendant of Ferintosh, the first distillery mentioned by name. This was owned by a supporter of the Protestant King William III, and was burned down in 1689 by partisans of the Catholic James II. The site is uncertain, but may have been at Ryfield, in the parish of Ferintosh.

Rights to distil seem to have been widely exercised in this extensive parish, which centres on the village of Conon Bridge, near Dingwall. Peaty, smoky whiskies made in the area were praised by Sir Walter Scott well into the 1800s, although the term "Ferintosh" was perhaps used vaguely in the way that Glenlivet has been. A distillery built in Dingwall in 1879 was renamed Ferintosh in 1893, but it closed in 1926, although its warehouses were used for whisky until 1980. When I took a look in the year 2000, the surviving buildings had become a business park. A name doubly destroyed. I remembered Burns: "Ferintosh! Oh, sadly lost! Scotland lament frae coast to coast!"

The shape of the stills at Glenmorangie, with their tall, narrow necks, helps create a delicate, yet full-flavoured spirit. Vapours that cannot make the climb fall back and are re-distilled.

SPEYSIDE: RIVERS OF WHISKY

The Black Isle is neither. It is not black, nor is it an isle, although its name suggests a certain magic. The Scots like the colour black: there are two distilleries named after Black Hills, and a regiment called the Black Watch. Perhaps black seems absolute, suits their sense of rigour. I wondered idly about this one morning in an hotel room on the "isle". Then I looked up and the window was framing the answer. In the foreground, lit by the sun, were fields of barley, golden and certainly not black; in the distance, I could just see snow on the peaks.

The "isle" is black because it is rarely white: it gets little snow in its relatively mild winters. Its summer sun seems just right for barley. As for "isle", that is nearly true: it is washed by firths on three sides.

The farms of the "isle" look across the waters of the Moray Firth and see more barley on the other side. The coastal strip there, known as the Laich of Moray, is a continuation of the same land. (Laich is Scots for "low-lying". Moray probably means a settlement by the sea.) The county seat of Moray is Elgin, a town full of grandiose buildings, where Charles Cree Doig designed churches, hotels, banks and houses as well as complete distilleries. Elgin also has Gordon and MacPhail, outwardly a modest grocer's store, but which has access to the world's greatest cellars of rare whiskies.

From the Black Isle round to the Laich of Moray; from Inverness eastward, past Nairn, Forres, Elgin and Buckie to Banff, and into Aberdeenshire – this is Scotland's barley-growing belt. Somewhere between Buckie and Banff, I was once taken by a farmer, a maltster and a distiller to admire a field of Golden Promise, the now-rare variety of barley that makes the silkiest, creamiest whisky. Its short straw also suits it to the sometimes windy coastline. The breeze was gentle that day. As dusk fell, the earth tones of the barley blended

Luscious barley (opposite, foreground) is grown on the Black Isle and across the water, by the Moray Firth. This inlet is fed by rivers like the Spey, which is lined with distilleries. The town of Elgin (above) is the administrative and commercial capital of Morayshire, and home to Gordon and MacPhail, a shop famous among whisky-lovers for its range of bottlings.

with diffused moonlight and a blue haze of darkening sky. The colours were as refreshingly cool as the dropping temperature. Some brewers and distillers feel there is a special freshness to maritime barley. That evening's aperitif malt was especially arousing.

An earlier writer on the water of life, Sir Robert Bruce Lockhart, speculated that whisky came from Ireland to the Western Isles, then found its way (through the Great Glen?) to the place where it can best be grown. This seems to make sense. The Western Highlands are fragmented,

Behind Gordon and MacPhail's unassuming façade, the bottles only hint at the company's treasures. It has more than 7,000 casks in its own warehouse.

rugged, rocky. This eastern stretch is easier to farm. The first impression is gentle, placid, idyllic. Thousands of miles away, the earliest civilizations grew forms of barley in flood plains, perhaps letting the ebb and flow of the water tease the grain into malt. Here, there are rivers enough to irrigate the Laich of Moray: the Findhorn, the Lossie, the dominant Spey, the Isla and the Deveron.

At the western end of this river country, the Benedictines of Pluscarden Priory, which still operates, once brewed beer; today's Miltonduff distillery is on adjoining land. At the eastern end, Dominican monks produced beer from the water that now makes Strathisla malt whisky, in the distilling town of Keith.

Barley and water made beer before distillation was

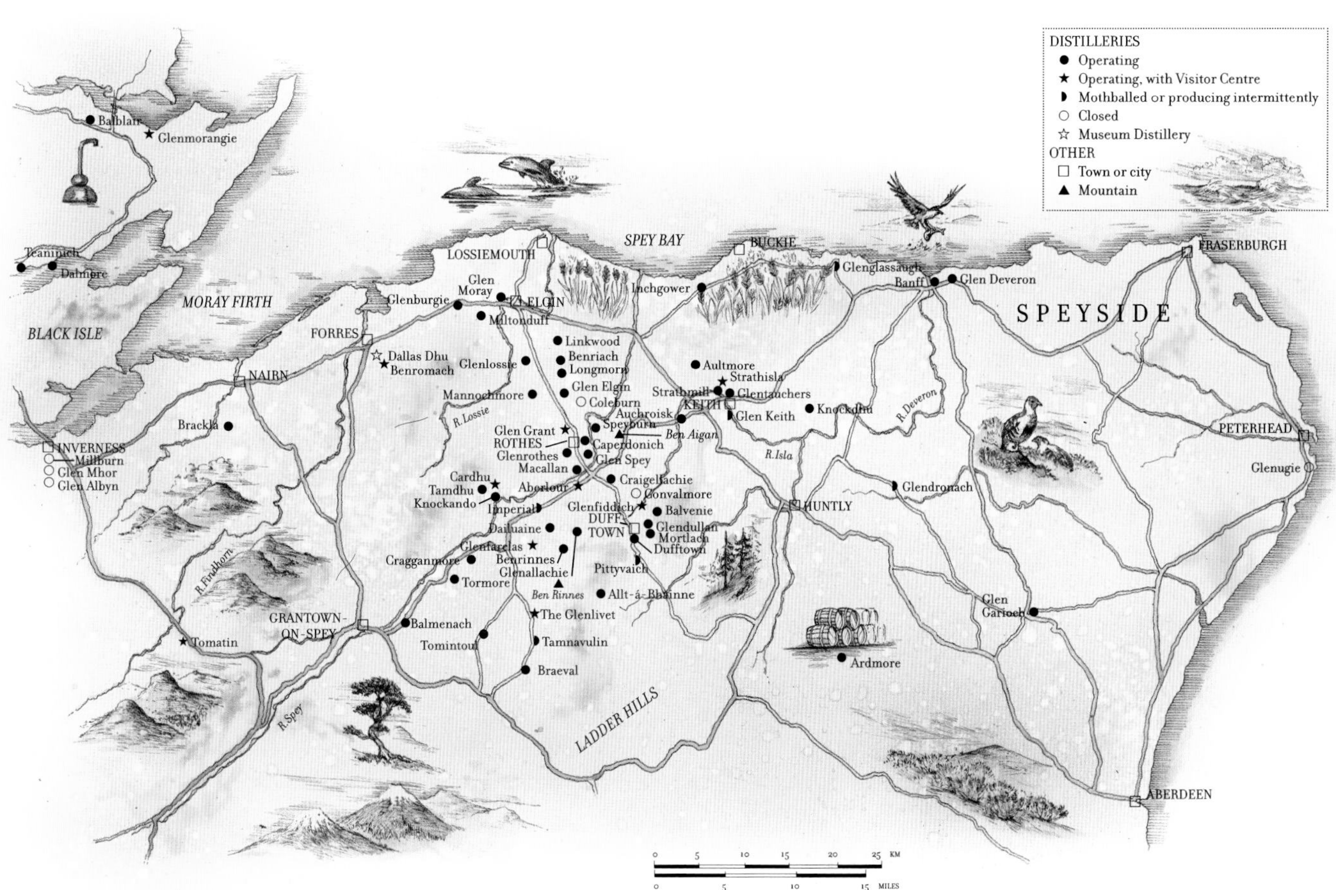

introduced, but whisky benefits more from heather and peat. The whiskies from all of these rivers are famous for their flowery, heather-honey flavours – and a light touch of peat, usually more from the water than the malting.

People in the glens of these rivers were making whisky long before it was legal, and their labours became an industry with the introduction of licences in 1824. Now, there are 50 or 60 distilleries in Speyside, depending on how widely it is drawn. Not all are working, but the majority are, some producing famously elegant malts.

One midsummer evening I went to the mouth of the Spey. It had been a good day, and it did not want to end. The midsummer sun was reluctant to sleep. It parted the clouds one last time, to cast light, salmon pink and eau-de-nil, on the waters, which swirled back and forth as the offshore currents tussled with the river. Bottle-nosed dolphins breached the surface. Four merganser ducks skimmed stylishly on to a shingle bank. Swans bobbed on the waters, nodding mutely. Herring gulls screamed blue murder. The osprey from up river had just scooped their supper, I was told by a birdwatcher, whose pleasure was heightened by my having missed the event.

Like me, the birdwatcher arrived by car. She had better have checked it had not been washed away. The seemingly placid, clean-as-a-whistle river is one of the

The sheep in the foreground are dwarfed by the broad sweep of the Spey valley. Behind are the hills that give rise to the river and its tributaries. On a pleasant day it seems tranquil indeed.

There's a hint of whitewater about the Spey, seen here in the heart of distillery country, near Knockando. Downriver, its force constantly reshapes the coastline.

fastest flowing in Britain. Its mouth speaks in tongues, dismissing and re-ordering the banks of shingle that form the coast. The river is "restless", explains a plaque nearby, recording some of its excesses. It is capricious, but loved. Rivers can possess us. This one exerts such a charm on the people who live by it. I wanted to experience the idyll, find the source of its whiskies – and perhaps understand its capriciousness a little better.

The Spey is rarely much more than 100 yards (90 m) wide, and just under 100 miles (160 km) long, fed by burns rising among hills of about 330 ft (100 m). It is not a large river, but it gives its imprimatura to the whole region and to the most elegant of malt whiskies. From the coast, there is a signposted walk 60 miles (96 km) upriver, with almost 30 miles (48 km) of side tracks, visiting the most famous distilleries. Someone ran the whole distance in a day, but most people take a week or more.

The signposted route is known as the Speyside Way. It climbs between hamlets with odd names like Boat o' Brig and Boat o' Garten, recalling the past importance of ferry crossings by coble, but it frequently follows the embankments, cuttings, one tunnel and several bridges of a single-track railway. For a century, the line took barley, coal and workers up the valley to the distilleries, and returned with whisky. The last whisky train ran 30 years ago. Now, only the odd stretch of rails remains, with trains for hobbyists and tourists. The little railway was the most fundamental of all the Victorian engineering achievements that elevated the currency of Speyside whisky from the farmhouse still and the smuggler's bothy to the landmark bars of the world. The ride must have been magical. The former track is fringed with an astonishing diversity of wild blossoms and plants, and often runs through lengthy arbours of ash trees. Small wonder that the whiskies of Speyside are so flowery, if they breathe this air as they mature in the warehouses by the track. It is as though the aromas are held down by the blankets of mist. These damp warehouses, especially those with earth floors, produce the most complex whiskies.

I began my walk next morning, with Alison Wilson, a ranger on the Speyside Way. At first, fishermen's paths thread their way through a braiding of wet woodland. Alison marvelled at the density of mares' tails in the swampy land. She sees it often enough, but it still reminds her of the rainforest she saw in Costa Rica. She pointed out the white flowers of greater and lesser stitchwort and a white blossom called mullein (*Verbascum lychnitis*) that looks like the foxglove. There were foxgloves, too, their purply colour matching that of the wild geranium called herb robert. Another purply flower turned out to be called the blue bugle. A truly blue blossom was the germander speedwell. The red campion seemed pink to me. So did the sweetly perfumy dames violet. And the buttercups that crept like strawberries? Creeping buttercups, of course. There were wild strawberries, too.

Only a couple of miles into the walk, I swore I could smell peat. It turned out to be the tar-like, resiny aroma of Scots pine. I began to wonder how much this omnipresent

The woodland floor (above) has its own herbal aromas. They add an appetizing, and sometimes surprising, element to the experience of the Speyside Way. Much of the walk is through arbours of trees (opposite). It is hard to imagine that trains ran here 30 years ago. The River Spey is only a stone's throw away. So are the distilleries. Glimpses of each make the walk unforgettable for the whisky-lover.

tree contributes to the atmosphere of whisky warehouses. The squirrels certainly enjoy the seeds, stripping the cones to the core. The crossbills are more painstaking, twisting off the bracts one at a time. On the floor of this wooded stretch were also wild sage and woodruff. "The smell of Scottish woodland. I love it," commented Alison.

She stopped to listen to the birdsong. "Is it a willow warbler ... that descending trill? No, it's a chaffinch. Less sweet." As we walked, we chatted about our lives. Alison likes riding, has dogs, and does a lot of work for her church. It emerged that her husband is a stillman at Macallan. Whisky is never far away on Speyside.

The path strayed from the river, as it often does, by the distance of one field. Suddenly, we regained the bank and found a ghillie's hut with a bench outside. I suggested we take a rest, and Alison asked permission of the ghillie. We sat down, and he told us that this was the site of Cumberland Ford, a significant crossing point before the battle of Culloden. The walk clipped Fochabers, where the aroma is of Scotch broth rather than whisky. The town accommodates the firm of Baxter's, famous for Scottish soups and jams, another industry based on the local agriculture of Speyside.

The route continues on a forest road round its first big hill (or small mountain?) – Ben Aigen, which rises to 1,542 ft (470 m). High on the hill, Alison looked back to search for the distant distillery of Auchroisk. We could not quite see it. The river was far below. We looked across at Rothes, one of Speyside's whisky towns. Through binoculars, Alison identified the Speyburn distillery from its fluttering saltire, the St Andrew's flag of Scotland. We thought we could also see the Glen Grant distillery, but we were not sure. It is possible to stand in the middle of the main street of this town and see none of the five distilleries, although all are just off this thoroughfare. (The others are Caperdonich, Glenrothes and Glen Spey.) The town's famous coppersmith, Forsyth's, is also hidden. The most visible evidence of whisky is the plume of steam from the plant where malt residue is dried to make cattle feed.

Round Ben Aigen is the village of Craigellachie,

Telford's bridge (above), at Craigellachie, links Morayshire and Banffshire, the two counties that embrace Speyside. It can still be crossed on foot, although the main road uses a more recent bridge nearby. The Speyburn distillery (opposite), at the end of Rothes, main street, hides in its glen. It is the prettiest location of any Scottish distillery.

named after a crag overlooking the river. Higher up the river, a second Craigellachie is a rock near Aviemore. These two Craigellachies mark the boundaries of the lands of Clan Grant, separate branches of which founded, or at times owned or operated, several famous distilleries: Aberlour, Glenfarclas, Glenfiddich, Glen Grant and Highland Park, among others. The village of Craigellachie also gives its name to a distillery, and is home to the Speyside cooperage, its yard piled with barrels. The Craigellachie Hotel, run along the lines of a country house, is a favourite place in which to accommodate business visitors to distilleries. Its bar has more than 350 single malts. Opposite is The Highlander, a small hotel and pub, with a smaller but well-chosen selection. I stayed the night at the Craigellachie, and set out again next day with Jim Strachan, manager of the Speyside Way.

The river is crossed at Craigellachie by two bridges. The older, built by Thomas Telford, is a symbol of Speyside. In a nation famous for engineers, Telford is the most celebrated. He built his bridge at Craigellachie in 1814 – "and did not have to wait long for it to be tested," as a villager explained to me, with a judgmental resonance worthy of the Old Testament. In 1829, the Moray flood, colloquially known as the Muckle Spate, knocked down every other bridge on the river. In 1992, the river rose 9 ft (nearly 3 m) above its normal level, and in 2000 a short stretch of embankment collapsed after flooding.

Craigellachie was the starting point for the main

continues on page 101

The coppersmiths Forsyth's, in Rothes, work for distilleries all over the world. In the smithy and its yard (left and centre), the bodies and necks of stills, and the coiled innards, suggest prehistoric monsters. Stills vary considerably in shape. Their design may originally have been determined by the space available to accommodate them, the construction techniques favoured by the coppersmith, or the views of the distillery's original manager or owner. Although the science is not wholly understood, it is generally acknowledged that the surface area and geometry of the

stills, such as these at the Glen Grant distillery (right), have a profound infuence on evaporation and condensation, and thus on the aromas and flavours of the whisky. Wishing to maintain the character of their own whisky, most distillers are reluctant to change the size or shape of stills when they have to be replaced. Stills are usually arranged in pairs, for the first and second stages of distillation, known respectively as the "wash" and the "spirit" stills. During the few hours of distillation, traces of copper sulphate are picked up by the spirit. Later, this will react with compounds in the casks during maturation. These reactions create spicy flavours.

section of the whisky railway, known as the Strathspey Line. It also had a spur to Dufftown, where nine distilleries have operated in living memory. The former railway meets an active stretch of line at the "silent" Convalmore distillery, near the thriving Balvenie, Glenfiddich and Kininvie, with the long-silent Parkmore in sight. Elsewhere are the working Dufftown distillery, Glendullan and Mortlach and the mothballed Pittyvaich. During a round of mergers among producers of blended Scotches after World War II, the independent proprietors of Glenfiddich became worried that their whisky might in

Both steam and fire are used to render the oak pliable in the barrels (opposite and inset). Fire is also used to char casks, so that the spirit may penetrate the wood and extract flavours. The craftsmen who build or repair barrels are called coopers. Much of the work of the Speyside Cooperage, in Craigellachie, is the rebuilding (below) of barrels from Kentucky. These barrels have already been used to mature Bourbon, whose flavours derive from the use of corn in distillation and from the vanilla-like notes imparted by new oak. When the casks are used again, the residual vanilla character is more delicate, matching the more fragrant style of whisky. Some Scottish distillers prefer sherry butts. Others balance the influence of Bourbon and sherry. The style of sherry, whether fino, amontillado or oloroso, is a further influence.

future be overlooked. Rather than relying on selling to blenders, they decided to concentrate on offering their malt whisky as a single. Their determination was rewarded, and theirs became the best-known malt whisky. Their beautifully tended, handsome distillery attracts more visitors than any other.

For the devotee of malt whisky, and perhaps for the lover of the river and its salmon-fishing, the most evocative stretch of the Spey is the modest climb from Craigellachie to Ballindalloch. Behind the crag of Craigellachie is the farm that accommodates the Macallan distillery and "château". On the other side of the river is the A95 road and Ben Rinnes – the second peak on the route, rising to 2,756 ft (840 m). Ben Rinnes is a Speyside landmark and the watershed for many distilleries. A 12-mile stretch of the gently winding road is signposted to a directory of distilleries, some at its side, others some way away: Aberlour, Glenallachie, Carron (which is the home of Imperial), Dailuaine, Glenfarclas, Cardhu, Knockando, The Glenlivet, Tomintoul … .

The river and the former railway track offer a more intimate view than the road. The old railway station at Aberlour is now a public park and tea-room. Tea and biscuits on Speyside invariably feature shortbread made in Aberlour by the firm of Walker's.

Snow on the Grampian mountains melts to feed the springs and burns that provide water for the distilleries and the River Spey itself. The cold environment of the mountain glens also helps in the condensation of the distillate.

Through the park and across the road is a tiny, turreted gate-lodge, built from local granite trimmed with sandstone. This is the distillery manager's office. Although it was once operated by a Grant, the Aberlour distillery was established in 1826 by the local laird. The history of distilleries on Speyside is tightly intertwined. In a famous gesture, the Laird of Aberlour presented two pistols to George Smith, founder of The Glenlivet. The gift suggested that Smith, formerly an illicit distiller in that higher glen, might need to protect himself against his previous colleagues. By going legitimate, he had deprived them of their smuggling business.

Today's manager at Aberlour, Alan Winchester, gave us a tour, then set us on our way, pointing back across the road to the local graveyard, with the tomb of James Fleming. He built the present Aberlour distillery and later rented Dailuaine, a couple of miles away.

At Dailuaine, the station sign has been newly painted, making the platform seem all the more forlorn as it overlooks the grassy former track. Dailuaine means "Green Meadow", and a sign there announces the "Biological Treatment Plant" of the distillery. It explains that "waste barley, water and yeast" are filtered through whinstone, and that fertilizer is recovered. The Speyside Way does not offer a view of the distillery itself, which in 1889 commissioned from Doig a more efficient vent for its maltings. A beehive-style vent was replaced by the industry's first pagoda, its shape designed to shrug off snow and rain. Its proportions were based on a "golden ratio" used

continues on page 106

Samples from different casks at the Macallan distillery. Even at the same age (top), they vary in colour. In the warehouse, a higher spot will be slightly warmer, affecting the level of oxidation (which, again, influences both colour and flavour). In dated "vintage" bottlings these differences are part of the pleasure. In bottlings identified simply by their age, an effort is made to maintain consistency by combining several casks to make one bottling. The whisky is still a single malt because it originates from one distillery. Earth-floored warehouses (right) maintain a damp, aromatic atmosphere, and mature the whisky slowly. In these traditional warehouses, casks are stacked only two or three high.

THE MACALLAN-GLENLIVET DISTY
3780
1988
THE MACALLAN-GLENLIVET DISTY
8793
1987

in the pyramids of Egypt and by Leonardo da Vinci. Sadly, Dailuaine's pagoda was destroyed in a fire in 1917.

We crossed the river by a bridge that once also carried the trains, getting a closer look at the distillery called simply Imperial, and built in 1897. The name itself speaks of the period. Then we were back among bracken and wild roses. We passed the former private railway platform for Knockando House, now densely overgrown, an indication of the past power of landowners. In the valley below, the ruins of crofts recalled the Highland clearances.

Suddenly, through the trees, I spotted the pagoda of the Knockando distillery. The well-kept buildings still have the crane that loaded the trains. The tall flagpole bearing the flapping logo of the Justerini and Brooks blended Scotch could not look less congruous.

Next, we came to Tamdhu station, with two platforms, a signal box, and mountains of empty casks outside the relatively industrial-looking distillery. Further up the hill, out of view, is the Cardhu distillery, rebuilt in 1872 by Elizabeth Cumming, one of the formidable women of whisky. This stretch of the walk should have ended at Ballindalloch, reached by a viaduct built in 1863. Instead, we continued for a mile, into boggy land, where the walk is made possible by stepping stones, so that we could admire the Tormore distillery. With its ornamental, curling lake and fountains, its belfry and musical clock, and its spectacular topiary, Tormore is the most elaborate of all distillery buildings. Surprisingly, it was built in the mid-20th century, in 1958. The architect was Sir Albert Richardson, a past president of the Royal Academy. It was the first completely new malt distillery to be built in the Highlands in the 20th century.

I had a particular distillery in mind as my final destination. Next morning, I set off from nearby Auldich with Jeff Charlton, a ranger for the Glenlivet Estate. This is owned not by the distillery but by the Crown Estate. We were now high enough and sufficiently cold for snowberries and cloudberries to grow. The Speyside Walk was still signposted, but it had narrowed to a track over moorland covered in bracken, blackthorn and heather, each of which had for millennia been contributing to the peat.

The peat underfoot had drained well and was quite dry. On the steeper hillsides snow had melted, then formed ice, and the peat had cracked and eroded. Sheep seeking shelter had scraped the side, leaving cliff-like peaty outcrops known as hags.

The heather, not yet in blossom, was nonetheless a quilt of different mossy yellows, pale and dark greens, greys and blacks. The young, green shoots, up to three years old, provide food for the grouse. The Gaelic name for the grouse translates as "heather cock" or "heather hen". For between five and ten years, the longer growth offers shelter in which the birds can nest. After ten years, the heather is burned to create new growth.

In July and August, the moister land blossoms with the pinky-mauve of the variety known as cross-leafed heath (*Erica tetralix*) and the drier slopes with the brighter, reddish-purple, bell heather (*Erica cinerea*).

From mid-August and into September, the purple ling heather (*Calluna vulgaris*) is exercising its hardier dominance. Ling heather can also be white, but that colour is relatively rare, hence its association with good luck. Ling derives from an Anglo-Saxon or Norse word meaning fire. Some distilleries used to burn a little heather atop their peat to add to the flavour in the whisky. The botanical name, *Calluna*, is from the Greek verb for to brush. The twigs were once gathered to make besoms. These were for household use, but were also typically employed to clean the washbacks (fermentation vessels) at distilleries. Heather's countless other uses include basket-weaving, rope-making, thatching, and the production of dyes and perfumes. Its aromas seem to vary, perhaps depending upon the soil, moisture and sun. Sometimes it is reminiscent of a sweeter lavender, often it is closer to honeysuckle, occasionally it is rose-like. A universal material, heather covers 4–5 million acres (1.6–2 million hectares) of Scotland.

On the ground, Jeff pointed out tufts of fur from a mountain hare. The fur was white, intended to meld with the snow, but the disguise had not worked. Jeff thought it had been taken by a fox. I preferred the notion of an eagle. Such discoveries were a welcome excuse to stop and regain my breath. I had walked only about two miles in an hour. Soon after, where the heather had given way to schist of quartz and limestone, we reached a plateau at 1,480 ft (just over 450 m). Jeff pointed out snow-capped hills 30 miles (48 km) away. Much nearer, over the next hill, was an odd sight: a plume of steam rising from what seems to be a steep valley. It was the glen of the Livet. The land where we were standing, the peat formations and the heather were all contributing to its water supply.

Soon, the chimney, and then the buildings, came into sight. They seemed very near, but were still two hours away. By the time we were in the glen and climbing to the distillery, I must have slowed us to a mile an hour.

The Glenlivet was the first legal distillery on Speyside. It is by law the only one permitted to use the definite article. Over the years, other distilleries have suffixed the term -Glenlivet as though it could be applied, as a designation, to any whisky from Speyside. That practice is now diminishing, although it has not quite ceased.

The Glenlivet was intended as the end of my journey. I sat down in the distillery's visitor centre and enjoyed a dram of the most famous Speyside malt: clean, flowery as peach blossom and delicate. I needed sustenance, and remembered on Speyside once being served Glenlivet soup. This was made from local grouse, hare and red deer, "laced with another natural resource from our region".

A few hundred yards up the hill from the distillery is Josie's Well, fed by a spring. This provides limestone-tinged water, which perhaps accounts for the firmness of body of The Glenlivet. The spring provides 12,000 gallons (54,550 l) of water per hour, and this consistent supply was a reason for the distillery's choice of site. Yet more water seeps through a hillside that is like a colander. The watered grass forms patches clearly visible from a

distance. A mile away another well provides still more water, which is softer. This is used to reduce the spirit in the cask from 68 per cent to 63.5, to aid maturation. The second well, between two ponds, adjoins the site where the distillery stood from 1824 to 1871. This is marked by a stone cairn. No buildings remain, although there was a chimney until at least the 1920s.

In the 1970s, the owners of The Glenlivet built a further distillery nearby, at a higher elevation. This was initially called Braes of Glenlivet, seeming to legitimize confusion about the designation. The name was later changed. It is now known as Braeval, and makes a light, flowery, honeyish whisky. At 1,100 ft (335 m), Braeval is the highest distillery in Scotland.

Three miles away, reached by Land Rover in a back-breaking ride over rocky tracks, a dam collects water from a burn that plunges from the Ladder Hills. The burn is filled with slatey-blue boulders, dappled with orange. I used them as stepping stones until the burn narrowed around my boots. The final ridge became a bit too steep for walking. A rustling sound, then: "Go back!" The order had a military clip: "G'back!" It was the echo of Scottish moorland and mountain, the imperious command of the red grouse, shooing me off its territory: "G'back, g'back, g'back … ."

The green shoots of heather provide food for grouse. The longer growth offers the birds shelter. In season, the flowers impart their scent to the whisky. These burnt patches, near the water source at Braeval, will eventually contribute to the character of the peat.

SPEYSIDE TO ABERDEENSHIRE

Heather is said to give its flavours to grouse and lamb, as well as to whisky. The finest lambs are reputed to be those that graze on the heather in the district called Cabrach, in the hills where the waters cannot decide whether to head north to Speyside or east to Aberdeenshire. The Grouse Inn at Cabrach is outwardly noticeable only by its lonely location, on a moorland road. It is an unpretentious pub, a traveller's rest and an accidental shrine to whisky.

I called in one morning to find landlady Wilma McBain busy. "Sorry, I can't serve you just now. I have to get some scones out of the oven." Within a couple of minutes, a plate of those scones had been placed before me, with a jar of home-made, rhubarb-and-ginger jam and a pot of tea. I was transported for a moment back into times past, when the textures and aromas of food were not sealed into submission by packaging. The tang of the rhubarb brought to mind a particular whisky – I couldn't think which – and reminded me why I had gone to The Grouse.

Suspended from every possible surface in the bar, and often in double ranks, are bottles of whisky, more than 200 of them, each upside-down, to dispense its drams from an optic. Thus is conspicuous consumption marshalled into correct and legal measure. Elsewhere in the room, and in the private collection of Wilma and Ian McBain, are 1,200 more whiskies, unopened. Ian wanted to give me a tour of his bottles: here was a bottle labelled "Malt Tonic" for the American market during Prohibition; there was a whisky made in China; here was a miniature to mark 50 years of The Grouse Inn. The pub was established in 1939 by Ian's father, but the serious collecting began only two or three decades ago. "What started it?" I inquired. "People kept asking me for whiskies I didn't have," he explained. "I thought I had better get them." I asked which was his favourite. "Oh, I rarely drink whisky. I am not much of a drinker at all."

Down the road from The Grouse is a small fountain, "erected with the surplus funds from a bazaar held to pay off the debts on six bridges on the road between Dufftown and Cabrach." Having dealt prudently with the essentials,

Over the hill, and into Aberdeenshire. The heather is in full bloom in July at Glen Muick (opposite and above), where a small river flows into the Dee at Ballater. This stretch of country grandly calls itself Royal Deeside. The heathery glens gradually open to wooded countryside, neat estates and aristocratic homes, including Balmoral. The best-known distillery is Royal Lochnagar.

a committee of civically minded citizens had indulged in a minor extravagance to provide visible evidence that no one had been cheated. I washed down the lingering maltiness of the Glendronach with a cupped hand of heathery mountain water and headed for Aberdeenshire.

There seem to be even more bridges across the county line: small, neat, humpbacked crossings traversing the rivers that flow east. On Speyside, the granite is omnipresent in the peaks; in Aberdeenshire, it is more evident in bridges, walls, buildings. The granite of the structures looks especially neatly cut. Perhaps there is less erosion from the weather, which is less windy. The rivers appear more disciplined and businesslike as they hurry along. "Aber" means "meeting of the waters". The two main rivers, the Dee and Don, have a job to do when they reach the coast: to frame the city of Aberdeen.

Aberdeenshire is a neat county. The craggier hills reluctantly yield to more rounded ones, with broad, sheltered valleys. The foraging, woolly-minded sheep stop wandering in the road, and cede the lower ground to Aberdeen Angus cattle, too well-fed and content to stir themselves. They do have to change fields from one year to the next, as barley is planted. This rotation, evident in the green-and-gold quilting of the valleys, makes for well-nourished crops. The mountain flavours of peat and heather-honey seem less evident in Aberdeenshire's few surviving whiskies, the barley-malt more assertive.

Glen Garioch, in the country town of Old Meldrum, is a typically neat distillery, with a clock that might decorate a public building. The distillery traces its history to at least the 1780s or 1790s, but most of the buildings date from the late 1800s. They are built in a granite that looks to have been flecked with salt and pepper. The past influence of a distillery manager from Islay led to the use of well-peated malt, although that policy is no longer followed. More buttery, flapjack, malty flavours are now emerging. A field of barley behind the distillery is a reminder of their origins. In 1977, the distillery ran short of water, and a diviner was hired. He found new springs nearby.

Glendronach, amid farm fields at Forgue, near Huntley, produced a characteristically big, malty, Aberdeenshire whisky. The distillery has been mothballed for some years, but its whisky is easy to find, with its teasing, sweet-and-dry maltiness.

Its less handsome brother distillery, Ardmore, with coal-fired stills, is a Victorian industrial giant incongruously marooned on a hillside. Its whisky, perhaps slightly caramelized by the flames, is creamy and malty. The distillery, in the hamlet of Kennethmont, is said to have been founded after a member of the Teacher whisky-making family noticed water pouring from springs on the hillside. Travelling by horse and buggy at the time, he was on his way to visit the stately home of a friend. The distillery has lived to see the rise and fall of the railway era. The train

Queen Victoria, who enjoyed the whisky of Royal Lochnagar, is reputed also to have appreciated this view near the distillery. It illustrates the neatness of Aberdeenshire, right down to the alternating colours of well-ordered crop-rotation.

Spruce and silver birch remain (opposite and above), but there was once much more woodland. Long-gone forests have endowed Aberdeenshire with rich soil. Beyond the wooded ridges, the more undulating countryside grows equally rich barley. There is big, but dryish, barley-malt character to some of the area's whiskies. This is perhaps a regional style, although the distilleries are scattered.

still goes by, but the station is overgrown and ghostly, with a traditional signalbox and semaphore signal.

Where centuries ago there was forest in these valleys, there is now relatively heavy, deep, dark brown soil. Rich soil makes for wealthy landowners. There are still spruce and pine woodlands, but equally often deciduous trees such as beeches, serve to screen private estates. Occasionally, unshowy stone gateposts, and perhaps a lodge, indicate a "big house" half-hidden in the woods. Where family estates control the land, it is planned tidily and kept clean, perhaps another reason for Aberdeenshire's well-groomed appearance.

There are many such big houses, and 150 castles, ruins or other historic sites. Several houses and castles are owned by various branches of the region's Gordon family, and there is Balmoral, the Scottish country residence of the royal family. The valley that accommodates Balmoral, and nearby Braemar, home of the most famous annual Highland Gathering, likes to be known as Royal Deeside. In Braemar, the local licensed grocer has a window full of whiskies and the discreet promise: "The Gathering of the Malts". The year's big event, popularly known as the Highland Games, and attended by the royal family, is partly sponsored by one of the distillers.

Balmoral's gateposts and lodge are plain enough, and the grounds can be visited at times when the family are not in residence. The castle was rebuilt in Scottish baronial style after being bought by Queen Victoria and Prince Albert as their Scottish country home. Shortly afterward, the then owner of the Lochnagar distillery, less than a mile away, wrote inviting the royals to visit. To his surprise they arrived next day, and the distillery subsequently began to supply the Queen. She reputedly drank the whisky laced with Bordeaux wine, thus ruining two great drinks. Royal Lochnagar, as it became known, is a malty, fruity, spicy whisky. Beneath the hill of Lochnagar, which inspired Prince Charles to write a children's story, the farm-like distillery, in pinky-grey granite, sits in neat tranquillity. It is a small distillery, but I have never seen one with more brass rails and copper piping. The piping is beautifully polished, and the copper stills cleaned to a pinkish blush, as though the royals were about to appear at the distillery again, which they sometimes do.

There was another "royal" distillery. Glenury Royal was one of the handful of distilleries on the coast. It made a whisky with a toasty, dry maltiness and some oily, aromatic notes. The distillery, near Stonehaven, in the old county of Kincardineshire, was founded in 1825 to provide a market for local barley in a period of agricultural depression. The founder, a local member of parliament, had a friend at court, to whom he referred coyly as "Mrs Windsor". Through her influence, he was given permission to call his distillery "royal". Unfortunately, that soubriquet did not protect it from closure in 1985.

Not far away, on the estate of the Gladstone family who provided Queen Victoria with a famous prime minister, is the Fettercairn distillery. This is on the edge of Fettercairn, an especially tidy village, entered by an elaborate stone arch. The small, pink, granite cottages contrast with a battlemented bank building. The pretty, cream-painted distillery, which dates from 1824, was rebuilt in the 1880s. It is surrounded by farmland. Its whisky has a nutty, toffeeish maltiness, but also an earthiness. Sometimes, I think I detect a note of chlorophyll. Others have found rhubarb. Time for another scone ...

The sheltered, rich countryside and the barley of Aberdeenshire. Some of the finest barley is grown in the area of the Glen Garioch distillery. This still relatively little-known distillery has its own maltings, although it has worked only sporadically in recent years.

DALWHINNIE TO PERTH

Geologists evoke the glaciated stretches of Baffin Island, Greenland and Arctic Norway when they describe one of Europe's great wilderness landscapes: between the Monadhliath Mountains and the Cairngorms, two sub-ranges of the Grampians. The scale is nothing like that of the North American wilderness, or even Lapland or the Alps, but the silver cloud, the swirling mist, the grey rock, the virgin snow torn by black burns, the dark earth, the austere grandeur, the emptiness, can be exhilaratingly ominous. "You can be filled with dread," a local person once observed to me. Many times I have expected the three witches of *Macbeth* to come flapping on the wind.

From 3,000 ft (915 m), the ice-scoured bedrock has been glaciated into steep mountain basins called corries. They are pitted with lochans that freeze in winter. Snow layers itself on the ice. The landscape is swept by glacial breaches, fanned by alluvial rivers. The waters rush over bogs that contain fossil remains of juniper and birch scrub, hazel and pine. On a less threatening day, it feels like being on the roof of Scotland for 250 square miles (648 square km). Whisky has to begin in the air before it can begin in the ground. This is where the first snows melt, where the waters meet the first peat. Snow has officially arrived in Scotland each winter when the morning radio announces that Drumochter Pass, at 1,500 ft (458 m), is unable to live up to its description. It has become impassable. This denies access to the roof. The burns that sluice from the mountains like rain from a gable, can, in a severe winter, flood a whole valley. The district of Badenoch (in the 1300s the base of a noble Highland raider nicknamed "The Wolf") is known as "the drowned land". This was where, in the 1700s, James Macpherson produced his

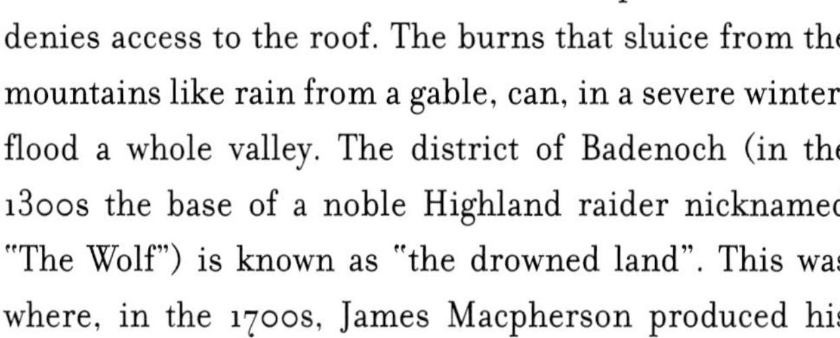

Under snow, the wilderness becomes so bare as to seem endless and daunting. It is hard to imagine such a dramatic landscape (opposite) in a country as small as Scotland. Amid the emptiness is the distillery of Dalwhinnie (above).

alleged translation of a Gaelic manuscript ascribed to Ossian, son of Fingal.

The drowned land inspires dreams. In the 1970s, a respected whisky blender, George Christie, drew up plans for a distillery, to be built by a specialist in drystone dyking. Work ebbed and flowed with the fortunes of the industry. The distillery took twenty years to build, and looked 200 years old when it finally opened in 1990/91. It is at Drumguish, where the tiny River Tromie flows into the highest reaches of the Spey. The nutty, oily whisky is labelled Drumguish. The distillery is called Speyside, reasonably enough, although this isolated producer is far from the region's cluster of famous distilleries.

An even more isolated distillery on the Tromie is Dalwhinnie, at 1,073 ft (327 m), in the hamlet of the same name. This distillery was originally called Strathspey. Despite its remote position, it is right next to the main Inverness–London railway track. As the train catches its breath, the yawning morning traveller can wonder whether he is dreaming, confronted with the twin pagodas of Dalwhinnie rising from a treeless landscape that seems to blend with the clouds. On a winter's day, the air feels as though it has arrived directly from Greenland.

At 9.30 each morning, the stillman tears himself from the warmth of his boiling charges and ventures into the

A distillery and a weather station, a wonderful eye-opener for the traveller on the morning train north. In contrast, the stillman must feel that his duties were ordered by a sadist.

The road east and south can be closed in winter. Once, it was a smugglers' track. Whisky made in the mountain glens, at first illicitly and then by legal distillers, was taken to Perth.

cold that makes his worm tubs work so well. They condense a spirit that eventually emerges as a whisky with a notably clean background and clear flavours, but that is not the object of his morning exercise. The distillery is also a meteorological station. Outside are a series of thermometers, one pushed into the ground, another on the surface, a third at eye-level. The average temperature is 6°C (43°F), rendering this the coldest place in Britain, although I can testify to sunny days there. If there has been any sun, it will have been magnified through a glass to burn a mark on paper, forming a scorched line as the Earth rotates. The length of the line reveals the duration of the sunshine. There are instruments to gauge the wind-speed and the humidity. Rainfall is measured in a simpler device: a Dalwhinnie bottle emptied of whisky. Visibility is tested by a yet more basic technology: how far does the stillman reckon he can see? The same technique is used to determine how deep any snow may be or how cloudy the sky. The whole procedure takes fifteen minutes or more.

Between November and February, there may be times when the snow is 6 ft (1.8 m) deep. Elizabeth Thomson, who represents Dalwhinnie in the British market, told me she was stranded in the distillery one Christmas. Did she have a good time? "Yes", she replied mysteriously.

Why build a distillery in such an inaccessible place? Wine writer Andrew Jefford suggested that the Victorian founders wished to pit man against nature (as so many Scottish engineers did). Or to test the workers' endurance (as though the work of the distillery were a Protestant allegory). Dalwhinnie means "meeting place", and the distillery is at the crossroads on an old, 140-mile smuggling route from the Spey to the more populous cities of the south. It must have been an even harder route with barrels or crocks of whisky loaded on to Highland ponies, over crags and tors, boulders and scree, bog and birchwood. The Forest of Atholl mounts guard over the baronial Blair Castle, which also has the services of its own private army, the only one permitted in Britain. I have twice been led into the castle between lines of rifle-bearing Atholl

Scotland's battles against bigger neighbours, and later alongside them, have made it a soldiering nation. At Blair Castle a private army protects, among others, the Keepers of the Quaich. "Do you undertake to uphold the spirit ... ?"

Highlanders, and announced by a man entitled Fear an Tigh. It has been demanded of me: "Do you undertake to uphold the spirit and aims of the Keepers of the Quaich?" I have agreed to do so. There have been rituals in the Red Bedroom. There have been banquets of salmon, Angus beef and Perthshire raspberries with heather-honey cream, each served with an appropriate whisky – dinner with 200 people in the Grand Hall, its walls densely spiked with 132 sets of antlers. High above, the oak beams are raised and angled like giants' axes. The bagpipes have howled through the narrow stone corridors and stairways. The mace has whirled. Lords and ladies, viscounts and knights have been introduced. The Earl of Elgin has

The arched beams and walls of antlers hang like a veiled threat over the celebrations, at which the Quaich is awarded. The rituals have a stern mystery. Would anyone dare not to enjoy themselves? Those honoured have included President Reagan, who is said to have been hesitant to eat the haggis.

spoken of "Our Dear Land ... this Great Nation of Ours ... wherever you are in the world, it will be a better place for your having been to Scotland."

The Keepers of the Quaich honours people from throughout the world for their services to Scotch whisky. Once the antlers have been braved, the village of Blair Atholl and the county of Perthshire offer Highland scenery on a more manageable, accessible scale. The Blair Athol distillery (which modestly makes do with one "l") is actually in the town of Pitlochry, a Victorian spa town with a festival theatre. The distillery, behind iron gates, was established in 1798, and has since 1949 contributed to Bell's whisky, which was originally blended in Perth. The distillery has been sympathetically expanded several times, and is beautifully maintained and landscaped. Its whisky is reminiscent of shortbread and ginger cake. The distillery's water flows from slate, graphitic schist and greenstone. The complex geology of these southeastern Highlands can make for dryish, spicy, textured whiskies.

There is a creamy mintiness, reminiscent of sugared almonds, in the whisky from nearby Edradour. The flavours are enhanced by the smallest stills in Scotland. The distillery itself is also the smallest, its whitewashed buildings tucked into a hollow. With its picket fence and white-painted wooden bridge over the burn, it is the most romantic of distilleries. It is also one in which it is easy to see how whisky is made, and it has traditional equipment. Edradour began as a farm distillery and was later a co-operative, driven by water power until the early 1950s.

Its neighbour Glenturret, near Crieff, is of a similar scale and style and perhaps even more agricultural in appearance. It is the only distillery where I have noticed a bicycle parked in the still house. The water is believed to rise from granite, and appears to pick up a little peat on its journey, by way of the River Turret, to the distillery. The whisky is sometimes peaty, often flowery and fresh. Much of it is sold to tourists. In Auchterarder, not far away, is the Gleneagles Hotel, opened in 1924 as a golf resort to bring business to the Caledonian Railway.

Between Edradour and Glenturret, and far larger than either, is the Aberfeldy distillery, in the market town of the same name, on the River Tay. The imposing distillery was built in 1896 by Dewar's, one of the great whisky dynasties. This was in the early days of blending, and Aberfeldy's whisky was intended for that purpose. Dewar's was an early blend and the first Scotch to appear in a branded bottle. The distillery's water, rising from whinstone flecked with iron and gold, runs through pine, spruce, birch and bracken. The whisky – oily, fruity and vigorous – remains a key element in the big-selling Dewar's White Label. This distillery, with an elaborate reception centre for visitors, is Dewar's showpiece, bursting with corporate pride. When whisky came down from the mountains, it first arrived in Perthshire. The famously entrepreneurial firm of Dewar's was originally based in Perth itself. From this "Fair City" swashbuckling salesmen like Tommy Dewar seduced the world with Scotland's water of life.

CODA: TO THE BORDER

For the whisky-lover, it is a pilgrimage. Immediately across the Firth of Tay, a quarter of a mile east of Newburgh, Fife, are the ruins of Lindores Abbey, which was founded around 1200. The monks were of the Tironesian Order, a reformed branch of the Benedictines. The abbey went into decline after it was sacked by Protestant reformers led by John Knox.

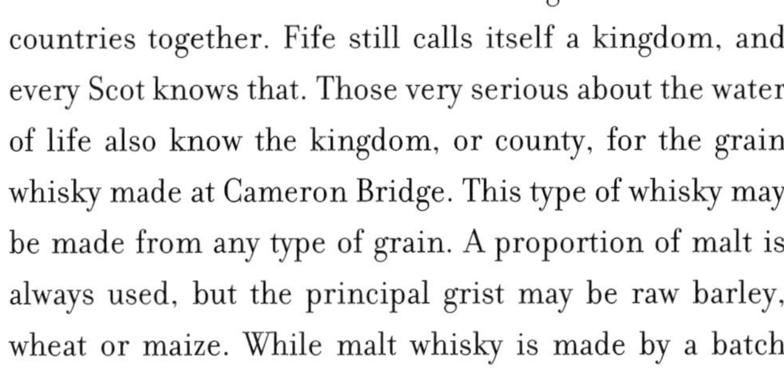

On a site of perhaps 150 ft by 300 ft (45 m by 90 m) , there remain about twenty fragments of wall and an arch, weathered and overgrown, but sufficient to identify its layout. One of its chapels has been dedicated to the splendidly-named, 3rd-century pope, St Dionysius. The private owner of the land lives next door. On one visit I knocked, and he allowed me to wander among the ruins and say a silent but warm-hearted, Dionysian prayer of thanks to Friar John Cor of Lindores. In 1494, Friar Cor placed on record in the rolls of the Scottish Exchequer the purchase of malt "to make aqua vitae". He was probably not the first distiller, but he gave us the earliest evidence we have. He was the first whisky writer. His brief testimony began my profession.

The exchequer was not far away. The kings of Scotland from Malcolm III (in the 11th century) to James VI in 1603, lived in Dunfermline, Fife. The latter Scottish king was the first monarch to rule over both his own country and England, although his reign lasted only a couple of decades. The crown was not enough to hold the two countries together. Fife still calls itself a kingdom, and every Scot knows that. Those very serious about the water of life also know the kingdom, or county, for the grain whisky made at Cameron Bridge. This type of whisky may be made from any type of grain. A proportion of malt is always used, but the principal grist may be raw barley, wheat or maize. While malt whisky is made by a batch

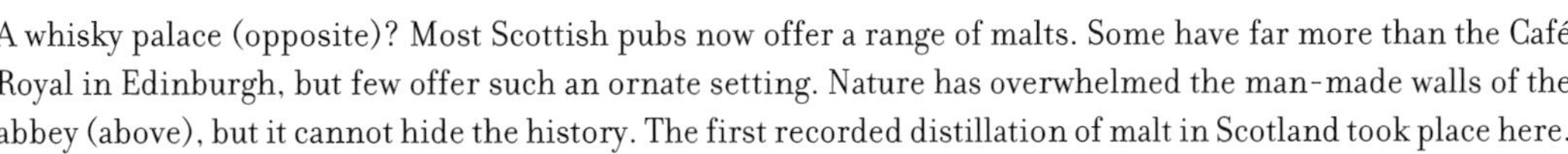

A whisky palace (opposite)? Most Scottish pubs now offer a range of malts. Some have far more than the Café Royal in Edinburgh, but few offer such an ornate setting. Nature has overwhelmed the man-made walls of the abbey (above), but it cannot hide the history. The first recorded distillation of malt in Scotland took place here.

process, in a still resembling a kettle or cooking pot with a chimney, grain whisky emerges from a continuous process, in a column-shaped "patent" still. It is distilled closer to neutrality, although it still has much more flavour than vodka, which is typically made from wheat or rye in a more exhaustive version of the same process. Grain whisky is aged for a minimum of three years – another difference, as most vodkas have no maturation.

Scotland has eight industrial-scale distilleries making grain whisky, primarily as the leavening in blends. A typical blended Scotch has at least 60 per cent grain whisky, usually more. Bottled single grains are barely more than a curiosity, but the abbreviated Cameron Brig is the oldest-established example. It is a sweetish interpretation, perhaps a restorative after a round of golf at the world's oldest course, St Andrews, also in Fife.

Scotland's most emblematic example of engineering is the 1890 railway bridge across the Firth of Forth. On the south side, the Forth broadens toward the port of Leith, once deemed not to be respectable, now bubbling with fashionable bistros. To be patronized in either direction might justifiably annoy the citizens of Leith, especially since their town was in the 1920s subsumed into that of their betters, the snobby Edinburghers. On a smaller scale, the social dynamics resemble those of Brooklyn and Manhattan or Yokohama and Tokyo.

Not only cities but also countries can be traditional rivals. The French had wars with the English, and thus made common cause with the Scots. For centuries, Bordeaux wine enjoyed its largest trade with Scotland, and was imported into Leith. A wine warehouse, which in part dates from the 12th and 17th centuries, is now the home of Scotch Malt Whisky Society. Members can use a club room and an apartment, but the Society's chief purpose is to find rare "vintages" of malt whiskies, bottle them at cask strength, without chill-filtration, and make them available by mail order. Most commercially available whiskies are reduced to standard strengths of 43 or 40 per cent alcohol by volume. They are then chilled to precipitate any natural compounds that might cause a haze, and filtered bright, a process that diminishes their flavour. True lovers of whisky neither add ice nor refrigerate, so their water of life does not become hazy.

Leith was for a time a centre of blending and warehousing. The Water of Leith is a very small river, more of a creek. It was in an undistinguished pub by the Water of Leith that I was persuaded to try my first malt whisky. I was eighteen years old, a foreigner living briefly in Scotland. I was unaware that a famous distillery had long ago operated in the neighbourhood. The whisky I sampled turned out to be a love potion. I did not realize this at the time, either. I simply enjoyed it, to my surprise, and desired to know it better. Its honeyed, nutty, earthy, smoky sensuality has now charmed me for decades.

Whenever I taste a Scotch whisky, I want to be in its homeland. I want to walk on the Big Strand, on Islay; or by the Spey; or stride the steep pavements of my teens, through the Georgian "New Town" to Rose Street. It spoke of sin then: a thoroughfare of pubs hidden behind the drinkless face of Princes Street. They said that no one could manage a nip of whisky in every bar on Rose Street and still stand. Everyone tried. Now that pubs are more respectable, there are paradoxically fewer of them. A notable survivor is the 1902 Abbotsford Bar, with its island bar in mahogany and moulded ceiling. Nearby, in West Register Street, the 1860s Café Royal has Doulton-tiled murals of inventors in the Circle Bar and stained-glass depictions of sportsmen in the Oyster Bar. This is said to have been the scene of a famous utterance by James Hogg, the Borders shepherd who became a poet: "If a body could just find oot the exac' proper proportion and quantity that ought to be drunk every day, and keep to that, I verily trow that he might leeve for ever, without dying at a', and that doctors and kirkyards would go oot o' fashion."

In researching the proper proportion, I often ventured higher in both altitude and social approval, to the neighbourhood of Morningside, to drink at The Volunteer (better known as The Canny Man's), founded in the 1870s and still in the same family. It is a sufficiently traditional pub to seem slightly eccentric today. At the time, it simply seemed to have beer and whiskies good enough to merit the climb. Edinburgh is built on dramatic hills, former volcanoes. Its urban walks are strenuous, but lovely, with sudden glimpses of the water. In that respect, it offers a parallel with San Francisco.

Locals advise against visiting during the overcrowded August weeks of the Festival, but they protest too much. From the grandest theatre to the smallest school hall or open space, every inch of the city is turned over to a play, reading or concert. The bars ring with comedy, tragedy and the clink of glasses. Anyone wearying of the performing arts can find a drink closer to nature by visiting the Glenkinchie distillery 15 miles (24 km) to the southwest, in the lee of the Lammermuir Hills. The buildings look like a Borders woollen mill, although the distillery grew from a farm. This is barley country once more, all the way to the border itself, at Berwick, on the River Tweed. The old county of Berwickshire is in Scotland; Berwick Rangers soccer team plays in the Scottish League; but, after changing hands thirteen times, the town of Berwick is now in England. That is a shame. The name means "a farm growing bere or barley" – the raw material of whisky.

In Edinburgh, the lights of Bennets Bar burn brightest at Festival time. The glow inside is provided by 100 or so single malts.

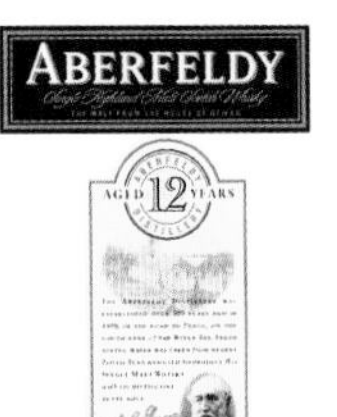

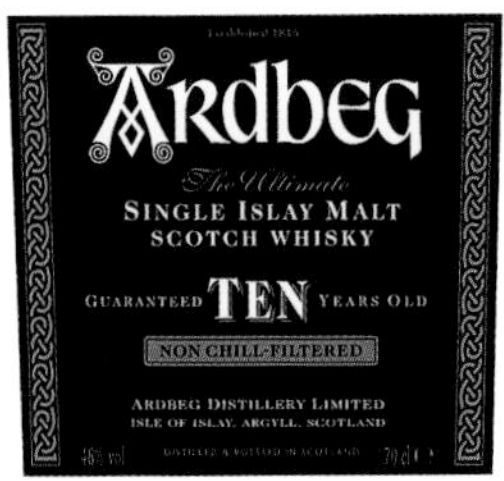

DIRECTORY OF DISTILLERIES

This directory gives details of all the working distilleries in Scotland, their facilities and their whiskies. It also includes distilleries that produce intermittently and those that have closed, but whose buildings still remain. (Some changes of distillery ownership were being negotiated at the end of 2000.)

ABERFELDY (p.125) Firm, fruity, lively, Highland whiskies made in the village of the same name, within easy reach of Edinburgh. A key component of Dewar's White Label.
Address: Aberfeldy Distillery, Perthshire PH15 2EB Tel: 01887 822010 Website: www.dewarswow.com E-mail: worldofwhisky@dewars.com (owned by Bacardi)

ABERLOUR Well-known and widely regarded Speyside whisky (p.103). Malty, nutty and spicy. Original buildings with 1980s flourishes, among more industrial structures. Visitor centre. Fill your own bottle.
Address: Aberlour Distillery, High Street, Aberlour, Banffshire AB3 9PJ Tel: 01340 881249 Website: www.aberlour.com (owned by Chivas Brothers)

ALLT-A-BHAINNE Hard-to-find Speyside whisky. Fragrant and flowery. Attractive modern distillery but no whisky warehoused on site. Its output is matured in the central warehouses of the owning group. No tours.
Address: Allt-á-Bhainne Distillery, Glenrinnes, Dufftown, Banffshire AB55 4DB (owned by Chivas Brothers)

ARDBEG Classic Islay distillery (pp.37–45). Reopened in the late 1990s. Earthy whiskies, reminiscent of rope, tar, salt and lemon. Current ten-year-old less smoky than past examples, but still distinctive. Whisky from a more heavily peated malt will emerge toward 2010. Restaurant and shop. Tour charge redeemable against purchases. Free tastings.
Address: Ardbeg Distillery, near Port Ellen, Isle of Islay, Argyllshire PA42 7EA Tel: 01496 302244 Website: www.ardbeg.com E-mail: oldkiln@ardbeg.com (owned by Glenmorangie plc)

ARDMORE Distillery (p.112) making creamy, robust Highland malts. Tours for trade only, by arrangement.
Address: Ardmore Distillery, Kennethmont, by Huntly, Aberdeenshire AB54 4NH Tel: 01464 831213 (owned by Allied Distillers Ltd)

ARRAN Newest distillery in Scotland (pp.24–6), on the most accessible island. Produces creamy, spicy whiskies. Open to visitors. Complimentary dram. Restaurant.
Address: Arran Distillery, Lochranza, Isle of Arran, Argyll KA27 8HJ Tel: 01770 830264 Website: www.arranwhisky.com E-mail: arran.distillers@arranwhisky.com (owned by Isle of Arran Distillers Ltd)

AUCHENTOSHAN Classic Lowland distillery using triple-distillation method. Grassy, lemony whiskies. No tours.
Address: Auchentoshan Distillery, Dalmuir, Clydebank, Dunbartonshire G81 4SJ Tel: 01389 878561 Website: www.auchentoshan.com E-mail: auchentoshan.distillery@morrisonbowmore.co.uk (owned by Morrison Bowmore Distillers Ltd)

AULTMORE Produces dry, herbal-tasting whiskies. No tours.
Address: Aultmore Distillery, Keith, Banffshire AB55 6QY Tel: 01542 881800 (owned by Bacardi)

BALBLAIR As a building, a classic, 1870s malt whisky distillery (p.83), in pretty countryside, north of Inverness. Enjoyable, delicate, fruity Highland whiskies. Tours by arrangement.
Address: Balblair Distillery, Edderton, Tain, Ross-shire IV19 1LB Website: www.inverhouse.com E-mail: enquiries@inverhouse.com (owned by Inver House)

BALMENACH A big, flowery malt, made high on the River Spey. Also bottled as Deerstalker. Tours by arrangement.
Address: Balmenach Distillery, Cromdale, Grantown-on-Spey, Morayshire PH26 3PF Website: www.inverhouse.com E-mail: enquiries@inverhouse.com (owned by Inver House)

BALVENIE The famously honeyish, orangey-tasting Speyside whisky, with its own small maltings. The distillery (p.101) is next door to Glenfiddich.
Address: The Balvenie Distillery, Dufftown, Banffshire AB55 4BB Tel: 01340 820373 Website: www.thebalvenie.com (owned by William Grant & Sons Ltd)

BEN NEVIS At the foot of Britain's highest mountain, this distillery (p.57), which is popular with tourists, produces whiskies that suggest chocolate and tropical fruits.
Address: Ben Nevis Distillery, Lochy Bridge, Fort William PH33 6TJ Tel: 01397 702476 (owned by Nikka of Japan)

BENRIACH Has not used its maltings in recent years, but continues to distil. The whisky, which is made next door to the more renowned Longmorn, has a cookie-like maltiness. No tours.
Address: Benriach Distillery, Longmorn, Elgin, Morayshire IV30 3SJ (owned by Chivas Brothers)

BENRINNES Uses the three-still system, unique on Speyside (p.103). Creamy, lightly smoky whisky. No tours.
Address: Benrinnes Distillery, near Aberlour, Banffshire AB38 9WN Contact via Dailuaine Distillery Tel: 01340 872500 (owned by UDV/Diageo)

BENROMACH New "micro-distillery" in the former buildings of a 100-year-old predecessor. Flowery, creamy whiskies from the old distillery are still available. Nearest visitable Speyside distillery to Inverness offering tours (charge redeemable against purchases).
Address: Benromach Distillery, Invererne Road, Forres, Morayshire IV36 3EB Tel: 01309 675968
Website: www.gordonmacphail.com
E-mail: info@gordonandmacphail.com
(owned by whisky merchants Gordon & MacPhail)

BLADNOCH Southernmost distillery in Scotland (pp.18–19). Restarted distillation in 2000 and hopes to maintain the whisky's distinctively lemony character. Tours. Shop. Complimentary dram.
Address: Bladnoch Distillery, Wigtownshire DG8 9AB Tel: 01988 402605 Website: www.bladnoch.co.uk (owned by Raymond Armstrong)

BLAIR ATHOL In the spa and theatre town of Pitlochry in the Highlands, but within easy reach of Edinburgh. This well-maintained, substantial distillery (p.125), makes cakey-tasting whisky. Tours (charge partly redeemable against purchases).
Address: Blair Athol Distillery, Pitlochry, Perthshire PH16 5LY Tel: 01796 482003
Websites: www.discovering-distilleries.com
www.malts.com (owned by Diageo)

BOWMORE Beautiful and hospitable Islay distillery (pp.46–50), producing fragrantly smoky, complex whiskies. Disabled access.
Address: Bowmore Distillery, Bowmore, Isle of Islay, Argyllshire PA43 7JS Tel: 01496 810441
Website: www.bowmore.com
(owned by Morrison Bowmore Distilleries Ltd)

BRACKLA, ROYAL Shakespeare enthusiasts will know Cawdor as a location in *Macbeth*. It also accommodates this distillery, making a fruity, dry, cleansing whisky. King William IV gave the distillery a warrant to supply whisky to the royal household. No tours.
Address: Royal Brackla Distillery, Cawdor, Nairn, Inverness-shire IV12 5QY Tel: 01667 402002 (owned by John Dewar & Sons Ltd)

BRAEVAL Highest distillery in Scotland (p.109). Formerly known as Braes of Glenlivet. Built in 1973/4, Braeval is an architecturally stylish modern distillery but has no warehouses. The whisky has a heather-honey zestiness. No tours.
Address: Braeval Distillery, Chapelton, Ballindalloch, Banffshire AB37 9JS (owned by Chivas Brothers)

BRUICHLADDICH A focus for local events, despite its "distant" location, Scotland's most westerly distillery, thriving under new ownership, is working full time, and making a wider range of malts. Visits: Monday to Saturday and by arrangement.
Address: Bruichladdich Distillery, Islay, Argyllshire PA49 7UN Tel: 01496 850221
Website: www. bruichladdich.com
Email: laddie@bruichladich.com (owned by Bruichladdich Distillery Co. Ltd)

CAOL ILA Connoisseurs love the oily, junipery whiskies from this Islay distillery (p.53). Tours by arrangement. Shop.
Address: Caol Ila Distillery, Port Askaig, Isle of Islay, Argyllshire PA46 7RL Tel: 01496 302760
Websites: www.discovering-distilleries.com
www.malts.com (owned by Diageo)

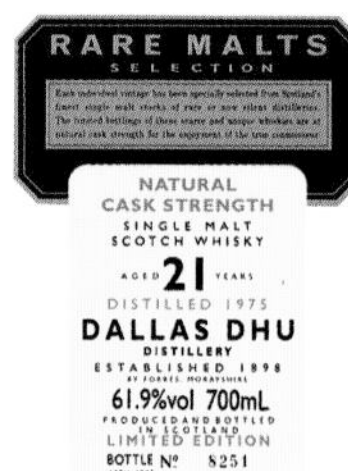

CAPERDONICH (p.94) In the Speyside whisky town of Rothes, opposite the better-known Glen Grant. Lightly smoky whiskies, with suggestions of dried fruits. Available only from independent bottlers, such as Cadenhead, Gordon and MacPhail, Signatory. Not open to visitors.

Address: Caperdonich Distillery, Rothes, Morayshire AB38 7BN (owned by Chivas Brothers)

CARDHU Easy to drink, delicate and sweetish, Cardhu (p.106) is the most widely marketed malt from any of the Diageo distilleries. The building is on the River Spey, in an attractive spot for a visit. Entry charge can be redeemed against purchases. Confusingly, the postal address mentions a hamlet and a village each of which give their names to nearby "rival" distilleries.

Address: Cardhu Distillery, Knockando, Aberlour, Banffshire AB38 7RY Tel: 01340 872555
Website: www.discovering-distilleries.com
(owned by Diageo)

CLYNELISH The most assertive of the mainland Highland malts, distinctly mustardy, though less aggressive than it once was. Handsome 1960s distillery (p.82) next door to its 19th-century predecessor, on the main road north between Inverness and Wick. Visitor centre. Tours (charge redeemable against purchases). Shop.

Address: Clynelish Distillery, Brora, Sutherland KW9 6LR Tel: 01408 623003
Websites: www.discovering-distilleries.com
www.malts.com (owned by Diageo)

CNOC (AN) The name in English is Knockdhu, which is easily confused with Knockando. Both refer to black hills. Its whiskies are creamy and fruity.

Address: Knockdhu Distillery, Knock by Huntly, Aberdeenshire AB5 5LJ Website: www.inverhouse.com
E-mail: enquiries@inverhouse.com (owned by Inver House)

COLEBURN Dry, fruity whiskies, still sometimes available from independent bottlers. The distillery closed in 1985, and there are proposals to develop the site.

Address: Coleburn Distillery, Rothes Road, Longmorn by Elgin, Morayshire IV38 8GN (owned by Diageo)

CONVALMORE Malty whiskies, still sometimes available from independents (p.101). This distillery closed in the 1980s, but it still stands. Its warehouses are used by the three distilleries which adjoin its site: Glenfiddich, Balvenie and Kininvie.

Address: Convalmore Distillery, Dufftown, Banffshire AB55 4BD (owned by William Grant & Sons Ltd)

CRAGGANMORE Makes complex, elegant, herbal-tasting whiskies in the Classic Malts range from Diageo. "De-luxe" tours, June to Spetmember inc., by appointment only. Entrance charge partly redeemable against purchases.

Address: Cragganmore Distillery, Ballindalloch, Banffshire AB37 9AB Contact via Cardhu Tel: 01479 874700
Websites: www.discovering-distilleries.com
www.malts.com (owned by Diageo)

CRAIGELLACHIE Fruity, orangey, nutty whiskies from a distillery (p.96) in the village of the same name. No tours.

Address: Craigellachie, Banffshire AB38 9ST
Tel: 01340 881212 (owned by John Dewar & Sons Ltd)

DAILUAINE Firmly malty whiskies from a distillery (pp.103–106) with an interesting history. No tours.

Address: Dailuaine Distillery, Carron, Aberlour, Banffshire AB38 7RE Tel: 01340 872500 (owned by Diageo)

DALLAS DHU The original Dallas is a hamlet on the western edge of Speyside. Its silky, honeyish whiskies can still be found, but its distillery is now a (non-working) museum, operated by Historic Scotland. Entrance charge partly redeemable against purchases in shop. Complimentary dram.

Address: Dallas Dhu Distillery, Mannachie Road, Forres, Morayshire IV36 2RR Tel: 01309 676548
(owned by Diageo; under guardianship of Historic Scotland)

DALMORE Produces Cigar Malt and rich, marmaladey, after-dinner whiskies in an attractive Highland distillery (p.84–5), north of Inverness. Tours by arrangement.

Address: Dalmore Distillery, Alness, Morayshire IV17 0UT
Tel: 01349 882362 (owned by Whyte and MacKay Ltd)
Webiste: www.dalmoredistillery.com

DALWHINNIE Famously cold distillery (p.123) in mountain country, high on the Spey. Clean, lightly peaty whiskies in the Classic Malts range. Tours. Charge redeemable against purchases in the shop.
Address: Dalwhinnie Distillery, Dalwhinnie, Inverness-shire PH19 1AB Tel: 01540 672219
Websites: www.discovering-distilleries.com www.malts.com (owned by Diageo)

DEANSTON Looks like a cotton mill, which it once was; the original was designed by Richard Arkwright. It became a distillery in the 1960s and makes lightly malty, nutty whiskies. Trade visits only.
Address: Deanston Distillery, Deanston, near Doune, Perthshire FK16 6AG Tel: 01786 841422
Website: www.burnstewartdistillers.com
(owned by Burn Stewart Distillers plc)

DUFFTOWN The town of this name has more distilleries than any other. The distillery of this name (p.101) makes aromatically malty, firm whiskies. No tours.
Address: Dufftown Distillery, Dufftown, Keith, Banffshire AB55 4BR Contact via Mortlach Tel: 01340 822100
Website: www.malts.com (owned by Diageo)

EDRADOUR The smallest distillery in Scotland has now returned to private ownership (p.125). Traditional equipment makes it easy for visitors to see how whisky is made. The building resembles a farmhouse, and is in a pretty Highland glen, not far from Edinburgh. Tours free of charge, with a complimentary dram of the creamy, minty whisky.
Address: Edradour Distillery, Balnauld, near Pitlochry, Perthshire PH16 5JP Tel: 01796 472095
Website: www.edradour.co.uk
Email: info@edradour.fsbusiness.co.uk
(owned by Signatory Vintage Scotch Whisky Co. Ltd)

FETTERCAIRN Estate distillery (p.116) in the farming village of Fettercairn, near Laurencekirk, not far from Aberdeen. Tours. Shop. Complimentary dram of the nutty, leafy, earthy whisky.
Address: Fettercairn Distillery, Distillery Road, Laurencekirk, Kincardineshire AB30 1YE
Tel: 01561 340244 (owned by Whyte & MacKay Ltd)

GLENALLACHIE Subtle, graceful, if restrained Speyside whiskies that are difficult to find as single malts. A component of the blended whisky Glen Campbell, which is popular in France. Glenallachie is close to the Spey, just south of its more famous brother distillery Aberlour. No tours.
Address: Glenallachie Distillery, Aberlour, Banffshire AB38 9LR (owned by Chivas Brothers)

GLENBURGIE
Oily, herbal, spicy Speyside whiskies bottled as single malts by Gordon and MacPhail. Most Glenburgie goes into the Ballantine blends. Trade visits only.
Address: Glenburgie Distillery, Forres, Morayshire IV36 0QX
Tel: 01343 850258 (owned by Allied Distillers Ltd)

GLENCADAM Creamy Highland whiskies, with a fruity complexity. The distillery, at Brechin, Angus, was mothballed in 2000, leading to concerns about its future. Trade visits only.
Address: Glencadam Distillery, Brechin, Angus DD9 7PA
Tel: 01356 622217 (owned by Angus Dundee Distillers plc)

GLEN DEVERON Sometimes known as Macduff after the hamlet in which it stands. The distillery looks across the River Deveron on the eastern edge of Speyside. The whisky is deliciously malty and clean. No tours.
Address: MacDuff Distillery, Banff, Banffshire AB45 3JT
Tel: 01261 812612 (owned by Bacardi)

GLENDRONACH It has floor maltings and coal-fired stills, but this handsome distillery (p.112) has operated only intermittently for some years. Its smooth, big, malty whiskies can still be found. Tours.
Address: Glendronach Distillery, Forgue by Huntly, Aberdeenshire AB5 6DB Tel: 01466 730202
(owned by Allied Distillers Ltd)

GLENDULLAN Big, peppery whiskies from a distillery on the River Dullan, at Dufftown. No tours.
Address: Glendullan Distillery, Dufftown, Keith, Banffshire AB55 4DJ Contact via Mortlach Tel: 01340 822100
(owned by Diageo)

GLEN ELGIN Honeyed, citric (tangerine-like?) Speyside malts from this distillery near Elgin. These whiskies are a component of the White Horse blends. No tours.
Address: Glen Elgin Distillery, Longmorn, Elgin, Morayshire IV30 3SL Contact via Glenlossie Tel: 01343 862000
(owned by Diageo)

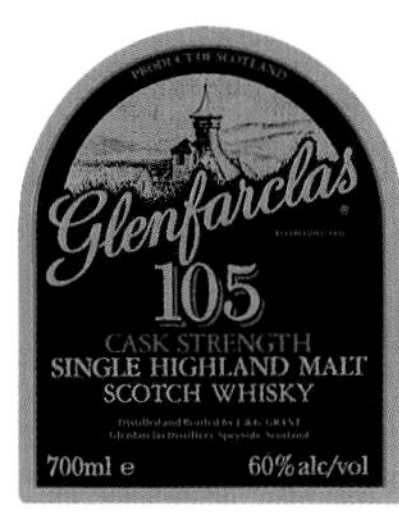

GLENFARCLAS Outstanding malts: big and very complex, with suggestions of raisins, almonds and crème fraîche. On the most densely distilleried stretch of the Spey, Glenfarclas is quite far upriver. Guests are entertained in a room with oak panelling rescued from the first-class smoking room of an ocean liner – testimony to the Scottish love of all things maritime. Tours.

Address: Glenfarclas Distillery, Ballindalloch, Banffshire AB37 9BD Tel: 01807 500257
Website: www.glenfarclas.co.uk
E-mail: enquiries@glenfarclas.co.uk (owned by J. & G. Grant)

GLENFIDDICH, THE The distillery that made single malts popular – every malt-lover should see it (pp.101–103). For many years the principal version of Glenfiddich carried no age statement, and tasted relatively young. It has now been promoted to 12 years old, considerably smoothing its pear-like flavours and adding nuttier, creamier notes. At greater ages, the whisky gains chocolatey notes. Free tours. Complimentary dram. Shop.

Address: The Glenfiddich Distillery, Dufftown, Banffshire AB55 4DH Tel: 01340 820373 Website: www.glenfiddich.com (owned by William Grant & Sons Ltd)

GLEN FLAGLER Linseedy, spicy, Lowlander found in very rare bottlings. A sweeter version called Killyloch was also produced. The distillery was dismantled in the 1980s.

Address: Glen Flagler Distillery, Inver House Distillers Ltd, Towers Road, Moffat, Airdrie, Lanarkshire ML6 8PL
Website: www.inverhouse.com
E-mail: enquiries@inverhouse.com (owned by Inver House)

GLEN GARIOCH "Old-fashioned", peaty, smoky whiskies were produced in this pretty Highland maltings and distillery (p.112) in the 1970s, '80s and early '90s. The malt used now is only lightly peated. No tours.

Address: Glen Garioch Distillery, Old Meldrum, Inverurie, Aberdeenshire AB51 0ES Tel: 01651 873450
Website: www.glengarioch.com
(owned by Morrison Bowmore)

GLENGLASSAUGH Grassy, flax-like flavours in a coastal whisky from Portsoy, at the eastern edge of Speyside. The distillery has produced only intermittently since the mid-1980s. No tours.

Address: Glenglassaugh Distillery, Portsoy, Banffshire AB45 2SQ (owned by The Edrington Group)

GLENGOYNE At Dumgoyne, in a very pretty glen with a waterfall, this is the most easily visited distillery from Glasgow. Creamy whiskies, emphasizing the use of unpeated malt and maturation in Palo Cortado sherry wood. Tours.

Address: The Glengoyne Distillery, Dumgoyne, Stirlingshire G63 9LV Tel: 01360 550254 Website: www.glengoyne.com
Email: reception@glengoyne.com (owned by Ian Macleod Distillers Ltd.)

GLEN GRANT The lavish, 20-acre garden behind the distillery (p.94) was largely planted by Major James Grant, son of the founding family, in 1886, at the height of Victorian interest in natural history. The tropical plants reflect his worldwide travel. A glass of nutty, herbal Glen Grant with peaty water straight from the burn, served in a "Zulu" hut in the garden, is a memorable experience. Admission Free.

Address: Glen Grant Distillery, Rothes, Morayshire AB38 7BS Tel: 01340 832118 (owned by Chivas Brothers)

GLEN KEITH Gingery-tasting whiskies from a distillery that has produced only intermittently in recent years. No tours.

Address: Glen Keith Distillery, Station Road, Keith, Banffshire AB55 3BS (owned by Chivas Brothers)

GLENKINCHIE About 15 miles (24 km) southeast of Edinburgh (p.129), the distillery is on a farm near Pencaitland. Among the exhibits in the visitor centre is a 75-year-old model of the distillery. The whiskies have suggestions of lemon grass and cinnamon, and a dry finish. Tours.

Address: Glenkinchie Distillery, Pencaitland, Tranent, East Lothian EH34 5ET Tel: 01875 342005
Websites: www.discovering-distilleries.com
www.malts.com (owned by Diageo)

GLENLIVET, THE The most famous whisky glen, hidden among the hills, close to old

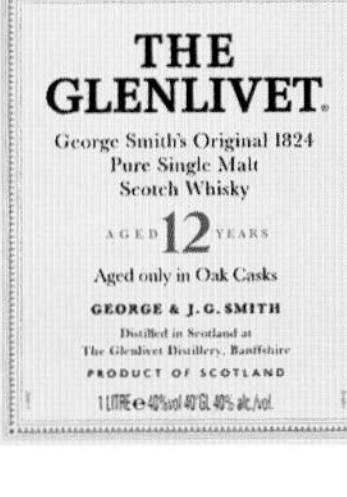

smugglers' routes (pp.107–109). At the distillery a former maltings has been elaborately converted into a visitor centre, which serves lunches. Free tour. Complimentary dram. The principal, 12-year-old version of the whisky is characteristically flowery with suggestions of peach blossom, but firm-bodied. Older versions are yet more complex.
Address: The Glenlivet Distillery, Ballindalloch, Banffshire AB37 9DB Tel: 01340 821720
Website: www.theglenlivet.com (owned by Chivas Brothers)

GLENLOCHY This distillery (p.57) at Fort William has startlingly elaborate pagodas, but it closed in 1983. Rare bottlings, with a toasted-coconut character, can still be found.
Address: Glenlochy Distillery, North Road, Fort William, Inverness-shire, PH33 6TQ

GLENLOSSIE Its whisky went into the once-famous Haig blends, but it is less well-known as a single malt. Flowery, with notes of sandalwood, honey and butter. No tours.
Address: Glenlossie Distillery, by Elgin, Morayshire IV30 3SF Tel: 01343 862000 (owned by Diageo)

GLENMORANGIE (pp.83–4) The biggest-selling malt whisky in Scotland is spicy and salty, but delicate, and always matured in ex-Bourbon barrels. For those who find it too light, the distillery pioneered wood finishes. Glenmorangie is a pretty distillery, set in woodland, and the best-known on the Northern Highland route from Inverness to Wick. Tours. Shop. Sampling. Small museum.
Address: Glenmorangie Distillery, Tain, Ross-shire IV19 1PZ
Tel: 01862 892477 Website: www.glenmorangie.com
E-mail: visitors@glenmorangieplc.com
(owned by Glenmorangie plc)

GLEN MORAY Chardonnay and Chenin Blanc finishes are indications of a more mellow lifestyle by the River Lossie. Witches were drowned here, and hangings carried out on the hill above the distillery. The premises are a mix of old and new. Tours. Shop. Sampling available.
Address: Glen Moray Distillery, Bruceland Road, Elgin, Morayshire IV30 1YE Tel: 01343 542577
Website: www.glenmoray.com (owned by Glenmorangie plc)
E-mail: tdavidson@glenmorangieplc.co.uk

GLEN ORD Barns of peat stand outside the modern maltings at this old-established distillery (p.85), close to the Black Isle, near Inverness. Malty Highland whisky, with a fragrant hint of smoke. Tours. Charge redeemable against purchases in the shop.
Address: Glen Ord Distillery, Muir of Ord, Ross-shire, IV6 7UJ Tel: 01436 872004
Websites: www.discovering-distilleries.com
www.malts.com (owned by Diageo)

GLENROTHES The aristocratic wine and spirit merchants Berry Brothers and Rudd of St James market this perfumy, complex malt (p.94). Behind Rothes police station, the distillery stands by a peaty burn, which flows off the hills. Tours are private, and by invitation only.
Address: Glenrothes Distillery, Burnside Street, Rothes, Aberlour, Banffshire AB38 7AA
(owned by The Edrington Group)

GLEN SCOTIA Fresh-tasting whiskies in the distinctly briny, oily, Campbeltown style. Tours by arrangement.
Address: Glen Scotia Distillery, 12 High Street, Campbeltown, Argyllshire PA28 6DS
Tel: 01586 552288
(owned by Loch Lomond Distillery Co. Ltd)

GLEN SPEY Light, nutty whiskies, but hard to find as single malts. A component of the blended whisky J&B, created by the London wine merchants J. Justerini and Brooks. The distillery (p.94) is behind imposing iron gates on the main street of Rothes. No tours.
Address: Glen Spey Distillery, Rothes, Aberlour, Banffshire AB38 7AU Contact via Knockando Tel: 01340 882000
(owned by Diageo)

GLENTAUCHERS Cloves, apples and raisins are suggested by the Speyside malt from this attractive distillery at Mulben, between the whisky towns of Rothes and Keith. The whisky was originally a component of the Buchanan Black and White blends. As a single malt it is available only in independent bottlings.

Trade visits only.

Address: Glentauchers Distillery, Mulben, Keith, Banffshire AB5 2YL (owned by Allied Distillers Ltd)

GLENTURRET This farm house distillery makes an unlikely home for "The Famous Grouse Experience", opened in 2002. Senses are suitably excited by this highly original, award winning exposition. Glenturret's very flowery, nutty whiskies are none the worse for that. Depending upon the age and vintage, they have varied from the pleasant to the charismatic. Records of whisky-making in the neighbourhood as early as 1717 suggest that this may be the oldest distillery in Scotland. Some of the buildings date from 1775, but distilling stopped in the 1920s then was revived in 1959. Glenturret has a statue to a distillery cat that was recognized as a world champion mouser by the *Guinness Book of Records*.

Address: Glenturret Distillery, The Hosh, Crieff, Perthshire PH7 4HA Tel: 01764 656565

Website: www.thefamousgrouse.co.uk (owned by The Erdington Group)

GLENUGIE The distillery was dismantled in the 1980s, although parts of the buildings remain. Bottlings of this whisky, with butterscotch, ginger and resiny notes, can still be found.

Address: Glenugie Distillery, Peterhead, Aberdeenshire AB42 OXY

HIGHLAND PARK The greatest all-rounder among whiskies, because it combines so many elements: maltiness, smokiness, heather-honey notes and sherry character, in a rich, rounded whole. With its own floor-maltings, the distillery is a classic, too (pp.75–7); it would be reason enough to visit the Orkneys even if the islands were not so spectacular in their own right. Tours. Shop. Disabled access. Coffee shop.

Address: Highland Park Distillery, Holm Road, Kirkwall, Orkney KW15 1SU Tel: 01856 874619

Website: www.highlandpark.co.uk

(owned by The Edrington Group)

IMPERIAL Big, sweetly smoky whiskies, made in the heart of Speyside, at Carron. The distillery (p.106), right on the river, has been mothballed since 1998. No tours.

Address: Imperial Distillery, Carron, Morayshire AB34 7QP (owned by Allied Distillers Ltd)

INCHGOWER Lightly salty coastal whisky. The distillery is near the fishing village of Buckie, not far from the mouth of the Spey. No tours.

Address: Inchgower Distillery, Buckie, Banffshire AB56 2AB Tel: 01542 836700 (owned by Diageo)

INVERLEVEN Scented, fruity Lowlander that can still be found. The distillery, in the Ballantine complex at Dumbarton, has not operated since the early 1990s.

Address: Inverleven Distillery, 2 Glasgow Road, Dumbarton, G82 1ND (owned by Allied Distillers Ltd)

JURA Most visitors to Islay take the opportunity also to spend a few hours on Jura, whether to see its breast-shaped hills, the residence where George Orwell lived briefly or the distillery (p.55). The ferry between the two islands takes only about 10 minutes, and it is a drive of 20–30 minutes round the coast to Craighouse, where the somewhat utilitarian distillery stands. The whisky has a distinctly piney tinge. Tours by appointment.

Address: Jura Distillery, Craighouse, Isle of Jura, Argyllshire PA60 7XT Tel: 01496 820240

Website: www.isleofjura.com (owned by Whyte and MacKay Ltd)

KNOCKANDO The name sounds comical to English speakers, but in Gaelic it simply refers to "a little black hill". The distillery (p.106) is on the banks of the Spey. Its whisky is a good example of the region's elegant, flowery-fruity style, with suggestions of raspberries and strawberries and cream. The outside wall of the manager's office is overgrown with roses and foxgloves and the garden has half a dozen varieties of heather. No tours.

Address: Knockando Distillery, Knockando, Aberlour, Banffshire, AB38 7RT Tel: 01340 882000 (owned by Diageo)

LADYBURN Dry, peachy, perfumy

Lowlander. The distillery closed in the 1970s.
Address: Ladyburn Distillery, Girvan, Ayrshire KA26 9PT (owned by William Grant & Sons Ltd)

LAGAVULIN This mighty malt is produced in a beautifully kept, handsome distillery (pp.37–46), with "rivals" Ardbeg and Laphroaig half a mile to either side. The fast-flowing burn at Lagavulin, and the seascape behind, neatly present the influences on the aroma and flavour of Islay malts. Lagavulin's whisky has an especially peaty dryness. Tours (redeemable charge). Shop.
Address: Lagavulin Distillery, near Port Ellen, Isle of Islay, Argyllshire PA42 7DZ Tel: 01496 302730
Websites: www.discovering-distilleries.com www.malts.com (owned by Diageo)

LAPHROAIG With its own floor-maltings, this pretty, well-kept distillery (pp.37–45) is a popular stop for visitors to Islay. They can view the seaweed lapping the warehouses, smell the smoke from the kiln and learn about the intensely medicinal flavours of this classic whisky. Tours by appointment.
Address: Laphroaig Distillery, near Port Ellen, Isle of Islay, Argyllshire PA42 7DU Tel: 01496 302418
Website: www.laphroaig.com (owned by Allied Distillers Ltd)

LINKWOOD Rose-like flavours in a Speysider much loved by connoisseurs. No tours.
Address: Linkwood Distillery, Elgin, Morayshire IV30 3RD Contact via Glenlossie Tel: 01343 862000 (owned by Diageo)

LITTLEMILL Lowlander with a marshmallowy maltiness (p.57). The distillery was dismantled in the 1990s.
Address: Littlemill Distillery, Bowling, Dunbartonshire G60 5BG Tel: 01389 752781 (owned by Loch Lomond Distillery Co. Ltd)

LOCH LOMOND Mint, menthol and eucalyptus notes have been found in whiskies from this distillery, which is in a former calico dyeworks north of Glasgow. Several variations are made under different names. No tours.
Address: Loch Lomond Distillery, Lomond Estate, Alexandria, Dunbartonshire G83 0TL Tel: 01389 752781
Website: www.lochlomonddistillery.com
E-mail: mail@lochlomonddistillery.com
(owned by Loch Lomond Distillery Co. Ltd)

LOCHNAGAR, ROYAL Near the Royal Family's Scottish country home at Balmoral. The hill of Lochnagar inspired Prince Charles to write a children's story. The pretty, farm-like distillery (p.116) produces whisky as fruity, spicy and malty as a ginger cake, especially the well-sherried Selected Reserve. Shop and tours (redeemable charge).
Address: Royal Lochnagar Distillery, Crathie, Ballater, Aberdeenshire AB35 5TB Tel: 01339 742705
Websites: www.discovering-distilleries.com www.malts.com (owned by Diageo)

LONGMORN Highly regarded Speyside whisky, with a tongue-coating maltiness and complex flavour development. The distillery is near Elgin. No tours.
Address: Longmorn Distillery, Elgin, Morayshire IV30 3SJ Tel: 01542 783042 (owned by Chivas Brothers)

MACALLAN This "château" farm and distillery (p.104), on the Easter Elchies estate, stands above the Spey, near Craigellachie, across the river from Aberlour. Tours are by appointment, and suited to the serious malt-lover. Casual visitors can drop into the distillery shop. The whisky, famous for its rich, dry-oloroso ageing, also has a distinctively fruity house character. Its devotees argue over which of its many ages best demonstrate its qualities.
Address: Macallan Distillery, Aberlour, Banffshire AB38 9RX Tel: 01340 872280 Website: www.themacallan.com (owned by The Edrington Group)

MANNOCHMORE Flowery, dry, Speyside whisky from a modern distillery. No tours.
Address: Mannochmore Distillery, by Elgin, Morayshire, IV30 3SF Contact via Glenlossie Tel: 01343 862000
Website: www.malts.com (owned by Diageo)

MILLBURN Smoky, aromatic whisky from a distillery that closed in 1985. The buildings now house a pub and a steak restaurant.
Address: Millburn Distillery, Millburn Road, I nverness IV2 3QX

MILTONDUFF Adjoins the Benedictine Priory of Pluscarden, near Elgin. The Miltonduff whisky is scenty and elegant. Trade visits only.
Address: Miltonduff Distillery, Elgin, Morayshire IV30 3TQ Tel: 01343 547433
(owned by Allied Distillers Ltd)

MORTLACH A classic Speysider, beloved of connoisseurs. Has an immense complexity of flavours. No tours.
Address: Mortlach Distillery, Dufftown, Keith, Banffshire AB55 4AQ Tel: 01340 822100
Website: www.malts.com (owned by Diageo)

NORTH PORT Dry, gin-like whiskies. The distillery closed in 1983.
Address: North Port Distillery, Brechin, Angus DD9 6BE

OBAN The town of Oban is the "capital" of the Western Highlands (p.58). Its smartly maintained, Georgian-looking distillery, faces the waterfront. It is one of the few working distilleries in the Western Highlands. Its whiskies, with a "pebbles on the beach" brininess, feature in the Classic Malts range of Diageo. Shop and tours. Charge redeemable against purchases.
Address: Oban Distillery, Stafford Street, Oban, Argyllshire

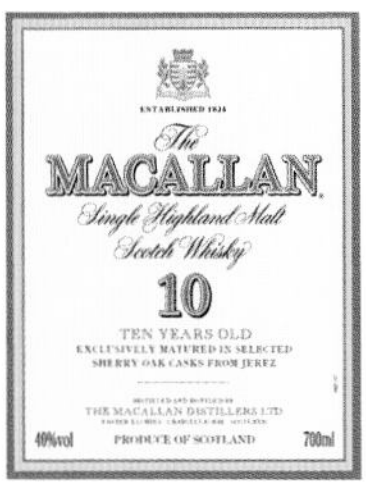

PA34 5NH Tel: 01631 572004
Websites: www.discovering-distilleries.com
www.malts.com (owned by Diageo)

OLD PULTENEY Northernmost distillery on the mainland of Scotland (pp.81–2), producing lively, salty whiskies. Tours & visitor centre.
Address: Old Pulteney Distillery, Huddart Street, Wick, Caithness KW1 5BD Website: www.inverhouse.com www.oldpulteney.com E-mail: enquiries@inverhouse.com (owned by Inver House)

PITTYVAICH Fruity, sometimes spirity, grappa-like bottlings. The site of the now demolished distillery is next to the Dufftown distillery.
Address: Pittyvaich Distillery, Dufftown, Banffshire AB55 4BR (owned by Diageo)

PORT ELLEN Whiskies greatly sought after as the very last bottlings are made. The distillery closed in 1983 but two ninteenth century malting kilns remain. The whisky has seaweed flavours reminiscent of bay leaves, and suggestions of olive oil.
Address: Port Ellen Distillery, Port Ellen, Isle of Islay, Argyllshire PA42 7AH
Website: www.malts.com (owned by Diageo)

ROSEBANK Flowery, camomile-like Lowlander. The distillery closed in 1993, but it might be revived on a micro scale.
Address: Rosebank Distillery, Falkirk, Stirlingshire FK1 5BW Website: www.malts.com

SCAPA Orkney's second distillery, which has operated only intermittently in recent years, although its salty, rooty whisky has a considerable following.
Address: Scapa Distillery, St Ola, Kirkwall, Orkney KW15 1SE (owned by Allied Distillers Ltd)

SINGLETON/AUCHROISK Attractively packaged, well-made Speysider: liqueurish, aniseed-like and sherryish, from a handsome, modern distillery. No tours.
Address: Auchroisk Distillery, Mulben, Keith, Banffshire AB55 6XS Tel: 01542 885000 Website: www.malts.com (owned by Diageo)

SPEYBURN The prettiest whisky-making location in Speyside (p.94), surrounded by woodland, on the edge of Rothes. Classic 1890s distillery. Heathery whisky, with hints of honey, fresh apples, cloves and marzipan. Tours by arrangement.
Address: Speyburn Distillery, Rothes, Morayshire AB38 7AG Website: www.inverhouse.com
E-mail: enquiries@inverhouse.com
(owned by Inver House)

SPEYSIDE Early 1990s distillery, looking far older (p.120), near the source of the Spey. Oily, nutty, whisky bottled under the name Drumguish. Tours by appointment.
Address: Speyside Distillery, Tromie Mills, Glen Tromie, Kingussie PH21 1NS Tel: 0141 613 3003
Website: www.speysidedistillers.co.uk
E-mail: info@speysidedistillery.co.uk
(owned by Speyside Distillers Co. Ltd.)

SPRINGBANK Great whiskies from the most complete of traditional distilleries (pp.32–5), which is independently owned: salty, coconut-like Springbank; earthy, peaty Longrow; and the more refined Hazelburn to come. Tours by appointment, (charge includes redeemable voucher).
Address: Springbank Distillery, Well Close, Campbeltown, Argyllshire PA28 6ET Tel: 01586 552085
(owned by Springbank Distillers Ltd)

ST MAGDALENE Grassy, aromatic Lowlanders. The distillery, which closed in 1983, was sometimes known as Linlithgow.
Address: St Magdalene Distillery, Linlithgow, West Lothian EH49 6AQ

STRATHISLA The Chivas Regal blends contain an influential proportion of this relatively robust, fruity malt. Chivas also uses Strathisla as a showpiece distillery (p.89). It is by the River Isla, in the town of Keith, at the easterly end of Speyside. A nearby spring was used by Dominican monks for the brewing of beer in the 1200s. The distillery dates from 1786, making it one of the oldest in Scotland. Visitors wander at their own speed, and

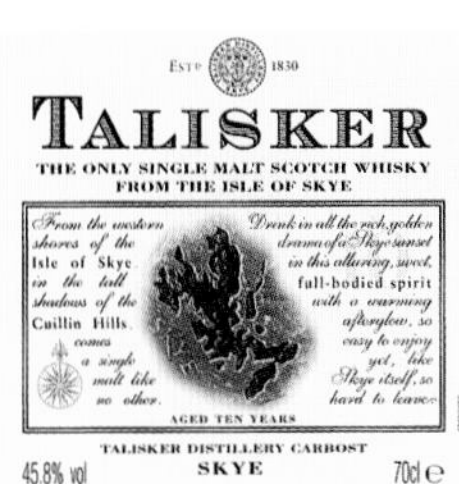

questions are answered by the stillmen. Complimentary dram and coffee.
Address: Strathisla Distillery, Seafield Avenue, Keith, Banffshire AB55 3BS Tel: 01542 783044 (owned by Chivas Brothers)

STRATHMILL Orangey, Muscat-like flavours in a whisky that is very hard to find. No tours.
Address: Strathmill Distillery, Keith, Banffshire AB55 5DQ Contact via Auchroisk Tel: 01542 885000 Website: www.malts.com (owned by Diageo)

TALISKER Skye's famous distillery, with its peppery whisky (pp.64–9). Shop and tours (charge redeemable against purchases).
Address: Talisker Distillery, Carbost, Isle of Skye, Inverness-shire IV47 8SR Tel: 01478 614308 Websites: www.discovering-distilleries.com www.malts.com (owned by Diageo)

TAMDHU Toffeeish, perfumy whiskies from a modern maltings and older distillery. No tours. Tamdhu is situated between Cardhu and Knockando, on the banks of the Spey.
Address: Tamdhu Distillery, Knochando, Morayshire AB38 7RP (owned by The Edrington Group)

TAMNAVULIN In the glen of the Livet. Confusingly, the location is spelled Tomnavoulin. This utilitarian, modern distillery has been mothballed since 1996. Its whisky is aromatic and herbal. No tours.
Address: Tamnavulin Distillery, Ballindalloch, Banffshire AB37 9JA (owned by Whyte and MacKay Ltd.)

TEANINICH Robust, spicy whiskies. This distillery (p.85) is near to Dalmore and Glenmorangie. No tours.
Address: Teaninich Distillery, Alness, Ross-shire IV17 0XB Contact via Glen Ord Tel: 01463 872004 Website: www.malts.com (owned by Diageo)

TOBERMORY Mull's pretty distillery (p.65), now with a shop and tours (charge redeemable aganst purchases). Complimentary dram. The whisky called Tobermory has a slightly minty sweetness. A spicier, peatier counterpart is called Ledaig.
Address: Tobermory Distillery, Tobermory, Isle of Mull, Argyllshire PA75 6NR Tel: 01688 302645 Website: www.burnstewartdistillers.com (owned by Burn Stewart Distillers plc)

TOMATIN One of the biggest distilleries in Scotland, and one of the highest at 1,028 ft (315 m). Tomatin is southeast of Inverness, on the upper reaches of the River Findhorn. Its whisky is malty and rich. Vistor centre, gift shop, free tour and complimentary dram. Disabled access.
Address: Tomatin Distillery, Tomatin, Inverness-shire IV13 7YT Tel: 01808 511444 Website: www.tomatin.com E-mail: info@tomatin.co.uk (owned by The Tomatin Distillery Co. Ltd)

TOMINTOUL Near the mountain village of the same name, which is a base for climbers and walkers. The whisky has a pot-pourri, perfumy character. Visitors welcome by arrangement. No charge for tour.
Address: Tomintoul Distillery, Ballindalloch, Banffshire AB37 9AQ (owned by Angus Dundee Distillers plc)

TORMORE The most architecturally striking distillery (p.106) on the Spey. Toasty, nutty whisky that is hard to find. Trade visits only.
Address: Tormore Distillery, Advie by Grantown-on-Spey, Morayshire PH26 3LR Tel: 01807 510244 (owned by Allied Distillers Ltd)

TULLIBARDINE
Situated between Perth and Stirling, the distillery has been mothballed since 1995. The whisky has a Chardonnay-like wininess, with nutty notes.
Address: Tullibardine Distillery, Blackford, Perthshire PH4 1QG (owned by Tullibardine Ltd.)

GLOSSARY

BARREL
In the Scotch whisky industry, usually refers specifically to a barrel of 40–44 gallon (180–200 l) capacity, made from American oak and previously used to age Bourbon.

BASALT
Type of fine-grained volcanic rock, which is dark in colour.

BLENDED SCOTCH
Blend of Scottish whiskies. Typically includes several malt whiskies with a larger proportion of lighter-tasting whisky made from other grains.

BOIL-BALL
Design feature of some stills – a rounded swelling at the waist. Said to help produce a more refined spirit.

BOTHY
Hut or cottage in which unmarried farm labourers, salmon fishermen or shepherds lived. Also, often applied to a building where illicit distillation took place.

BOURBON
American whiskey, historically associated with Bourbon County, Kentucky.

BURN
Scots word for a small stream or brook.

BUTT
Sherry cask used in the maturation of whisky. Has a capacity of 110 gallons (500 l).

CAIRN (Gaelic origin)
Mound of stones, sometimes pyramid-shaped, erected as a monument or landmark.

CASK
In the whisky industry, a generic term for a wooden vessel used in the maturation of whisky. (The terms barrel, butt and hogshead have more specific meanings.)

CEILIDH (Gaelic)
Pronounced *kaily*. Social gathering, usually with music and dancing.

CHILL-FILTRATION
Most producers chill their whisky to precipitate fatty acids and proteins, then filter it before bottling. The absence of these elements ensures that the whisky will not cloud when it is reduced in strength by the addition of water, or if the consumer adds ice to the drink. Unfortunately, chill-filtration also removes some body, texture and flavour.

CLOUDBERRY (*Rubus chamaemorus*)
Mountain shrub with a white flower. Bears orange-coloured fruit.

CROFT
Very small holding of land, usually rented and tended by one individual or family.

DRAM
Scottish term for a drink – almost always whisky. Often understood to mean a double measure. Also, a free allowance once given to distillery workers. Possibly of Gaelic origin, or from the Greek *drachma*.

DRUMLIN (Gaelic origin)
Oval mound formed by glaciation.

ESTER
Often fragrant, fruity or spicy compound created by reactions in fermentation or maturation.

FIRTH
A sheltered inlet or arm of the sea.

FLAPJACK
Oatcake sweetened with syrup and demerara sugar. Made in slabs and served in slices.

GHILLIE, GILLIE (Gaelic)
Originally, the attendant to a Highland chief. Now, a person who guides and assists enthusiasts in salmon fishing or deer stalking.

GLEN
Narrow valley, usually with a river.

HAGGIS
Dish most associated with Scotland: a sheep's stomach stuffed with lamb's or deer's liver, offal, oatmeal, etc. Well-seasoned and traditionally moistened with whisky.

HOGSHEAD
Cask with a capacity of 55 gallons (250 l), traditionally favoured in the malt-whisky industry. Often rebuilt from American barrel staves.

LADE
Channel dug to direct water to a distillery or mill.

LAIRD
Today, refers to the lord of the manor. Historically, a chieftain or a prince.

LOCH
Usually a lake; or an inlet, largely enclosed from the sea.

LOCHAN
Small loch or pond.

LYNE ARM
The tube that carries vapour from the still to the condenser.

MALT
Grain that has been steeped, partially germinated, and dried in a kiln to render it soluble. The person who carries out this work is a maltster. The building where it happens is a maltings.

MALT WHISKY
Whisky made from malted barley, and no other grain.

MASH
Verb: To mix malt with warm water to release fermentable sugars. Noun: the mixture. Mash-tun (see TUN) is the vessel in which this process takes place.

MUCKLE
Scots word meaning great or big.

QUAICH
Possibly derived from the Gaelic *cuach*, and related to "cup". Or from "keg", which has Scandinavian origins. A quaich is a two-handled vessel for the (often ceremonial) serving of whisky.

SCHIST
Rock comprising different minerals interleaved. Often flaky.

SCOTCH
Whisky made in Scotland and matured there for at least three years.

SINGLE MALT
Malt whisky that is the product of a single distillery.

SNOWBERRY (*Symphoricarpos albus*)
Shrub with a pink flower and a large white berry.

SPATE
Heavy rain or flood.

STILL
Kettle-like vessel used to distil.

TUN
Old term for a large, fixed vessel. Used today in "mash-tun". In the past, fermenting vessels may have also been known as "tuns". Hence "tun room" is the fermenting area.

WASH
Fermenting, or fermented, solution of malt sugars.

WASH-BACK
Fermenting vessel.

WHIN
Scottish name for gorse.

WHISKY
Matured spirit drink first made in Ireland and Scotland. Produced from grain, usually including barley malt, and retaining aromas and flavours from the raw material.

WORM TUB
Traditional condenser, in which vapour passes through a copper coil (or "worm") submerged in cold water. The modern condenser uses multiple, straight tubes.

WORT
Solution of malt sugars, before yeast is added. Once the yeast is added, it starts to ferment and becomes wash (see above).

INDEX

NOTE: Entries in the Directory (pp.130–39) have not been indexed.

AUTHOR'S ACKNOWLEDGMENTS

In writing my books on whisky over the decades, I have been grateful for the help of every distillery and owning company. Specifically for their help on this book, my thanks to: Eddie Aldridge; Raymond Armstrong; Rachel Barrie; Jane Beechey and BMA PR; Steve Blake; Billy Bun; Trisha Booth and Phipps PR; Dr John Brown; Jeff Charlton; Jim Cryle; Harold Currie; Robin Dods; Duncan Elphick and the staff of the Craigellachie Hotel; William Gordon; Lynne Grant; Alan Greig; Jane Hunter; Mark Lawson; Dr Bill Lumsden; Cathie Macleod; Graham MacWilliam; Jim McEwan; Frank McHardy; Gordon and Margaret McIntosh; Gordon Mitchell; Martine Nouet; Pauline Ogilvie; Geoff Palmer; Richard Paterson; Andrew Patterson; David Robertson; Colin Ross; Jacqui Stacy; David Stewart; Dr Margaret Storrie; Jim Strachan; Alison Wilson; and Alan Winchester, among many others.

I would also like the thank the authors and publishers of the following titles, which I consulted during the creation of this book: *The Scotch Whisky Industry Record* by Charles Craig; *Whisky on the Rocks* by Stephen and Julie Cribb; The Living Landscapes series (Scottish Natural Heritage); *Introducing Heather* by David Lambie; *Scotland's Place-names* by David Dorward; *The Pocket Scots Dictionary* (Polygon); *Scottish Islands* by Hamish Haswell-Smith; *The Isles* by Norman Davies.